Water and Instability in the Middle East

INTRODUCTION

Anxiety over dwindling water supplies in the Middle East has been widely tipped as the next cause of conflict in the region. However, a closer examination of this view reveals it to be seriously misleading. It masks the complexity of water-resource management on a national and international level and overlooks the efforts which are being made to avoid conflict which, Middle East governments agree, cannot resolve the water crisis in the long term. The crisis relates fundamentally to the nature of water allocation and use within states rather than to water allocation between states. However, it is current and possible future disputes over shared water resources which attract attention and present a sensational image of instability.

There has been a proliferation of alarmist predictions. A number of recent studies have suggested that water shortages in the Middle East will intensify and aggravate competition between states, leading to 'unprecedented upheavals'. Disputes over water distribution are likely, it is suggested, to lead to armed conflict, while water could become more valuable than oil as a strategic asset. Salameh concluded: 'the Middle East is living on a time bomb. It could explode at any time'.[1] These studies focus very much on the role of water in international relations, giving water a degree of strategic prominence which it does not necessarily merit.

This Paper aims to analyse the context in which water issues may or may not lead to inter-state conflict or internal unrest, and to what extent they mitigate or aggravate other factors of conflict. The Paper deals specifically with the states of the Middle East and North Africa that share surface or ground-water with their neighbours (i.e., those in the three main river basin systems: the Jordan and the Litani; the Tigris and Euphrates; and the Nile). Past water-related controversies are identified and prospects for conflict or negotiated solutions are assessed. In addition, the Paper examines the objectives of water planning within the context of national economic priorities, since this is the key to understanding the importance of water in the international arena.

The water crisis in the Middle East is attributable to three sets of factors: environmental, economic and political. Annual water supply in the region is neither reliable nor plentiful; the climate is largely arid or semi-arid with average annual rainfall levels of less than 250mm/yr, except on the Mediterranean coast and upland areas of Lebanon, Syria and Iraq. Only Turkey and Iran enjoy a relative water surplus. Water

3

available from renewable sources (rivers, lakes, springs and rechargeable ground-water) and from non-renewable fossil ground-water cannot keep pace with demand, as populations in all states of the region are expanding rapidly at an average annual rate of 2.2–3.7%. The winter of 1991–2 was one of the coldest and wettest on record, bringing heavy rains and snowfalls to Jordan and Israel, the most water deficient states in the region, but it provided little more than a temporary respite after several years of drought.

Over 70% of water supplies in the Middle East are allocated to irrigated agriculture (which in arid lands requires a minimum annual water depth of 1–1.6 metres) to increase crop yields and the number of crops which can be cultivated in a growing season. Yet the importance of the agricultural sector to national income generation and employment is declining steadily in all countries except Turkey and Sudan (see Tables 2 and 3 on pp. 74–75). Despite falling productivity in most cases and widespread drought, government investment in dam and irrigation projects and in the cultivation of cereal crops increased throughout the 1980s, motivated by fears of growing dependence on food imports. Many Middle Eastern governments have been actively promoting a policy of food security and self-reliance as a national economic goal. However, food security is primarily a political and social policy objective which is pursued despite poor economic returns. The policy favours certain interest groups, and the influence of pro-agricultural and related engineering lobbies should not be underestimated. For instance, in Israel, farmers have formed a strong political pressure group. In Syria, priority has been given to irrigation in the Euphrates valley, which is also a major recruiting ground for the armed forces, while in Egypt veterans of the 1973 Arab–Israeli war were given plots of reclaimed land designated for increased food crop cultivation despite their lack of farming expertise. In Libya, one of the principal objectives of the Great Man-Made River project (see Appendix 1 on p. 72) is to supply water for irrigation and other uses in the Sirte region, which is outside the traditionally cultivated zone but is Libyan leader Colonel Gaddafi's family home area. The Iraqi government has embarked on a plan to build a 'third river' between the Tigris and the Euphrates, ostensibly to rehabilitate large areas of degraded agricultural land but also to drain marshland areas which have provided a haven for opponents to Saddam Hussein's regime. The marginal value added of water (if water is costed as an input) in agriculture is low compared to that in other sectors of the economy, but pressures within many Middle Eastern states for substantial budgetary allocations to agriculture persist, regardless of performance. The policy of food security is consequently a tremendous drain on limited water budgets (see Appendix 1 on p. 72).

On the other hand, maintaining or expanding agricultural production is justifiable according to different socioeconomic criteria, such as slowing the trend of rural–urban migration, or creating

4

regional growth poles and easing pressure on existing population centres. Investment in irrigation projects creates employment and provides markets for other economic sectors, while high-value crops may generate appreciable foreign-exchange revenues. Nevertheless, in many cases agricultural policy has suffered from insufficient investment in extension facilities (the provision of seeds, fertilisers, veterinary services and credit), marketing and training.

Water has, so far, not been treated as a valuable commodity but, to a great extent, as a free gift of nature. Farmers in particular have tended to enjoy substantial water subsidies in the Middle East, and in some areas, such as the Nile valley and delta in Egypt, receive water virtually free of charge (they are indirectly charged through the regulation and pricing of cotton). Although international funding agencies and many local technocrats regard water pricing as a useful tool for regulating consumption, it is an extremely sensitive issue politically and where it has been implemented regulations have been widely flouted. Pricing water on a volumetric basis requires a great deal of infrastructure and administration: the installation and regular maintenance of water meters, designating peak demand periods and minimum quality standards and regulating demand by imposing penalties for excessive use. On a national level, water-management policy is often left to competing agencies and bureaucracies; more than one hydraulic project in the Middle East has run into difficulties because of the widely differing expectations of planners and beneficiaries.

Water conservation is now on the national agenda of many states in the region and, amidst gloomy forecasts of growing supply–demand disparities, the search continues for 'new water': tapping reserves of fossil water; recycling waste water as well as brackish and sea-water desalination; and introducing more efficient water delivery systems for irrigation and municipal networks. Modernizing irrigation systems can make a tremendous impact on national water budgets. The most widely-used system in the region is still surface irrigation which has a 40–50% efficiency rate. Sprinkler and drip irrigation methods (which have a 65–75% and 90% rate of efficiency, respectively) are widely used in Israel, Jordan and the Gulf states, but are far more expensive to install and maintain and need to be operated by trained personnel. The economic advantages of water-saving are considerable, however. It is estimated that the cost of saving one cubic metre of water is usually lower than the marginal cost of producing water from an alternative source.[2]

In the field of international relations, all of these environmental factors and technological developments are overshadowed by political issues, including the Arab–Israeli conflict, the Kurdish question and the fluidity of political alliances in the Horn of Africa. Water management has become politicized through the sharing by two or more states of regional surface and ground-water resources. Tension is inevitable if upstream states on international rivers embark on pro-

5

jects which reduce the flow of water downstream, or if ground-water abstraction in one state leads to appreciable reduction in the water table in neighbouring states.

The consultative process is also inadequate: there is no satisfactory body of international law to deal with the issue of shared water courses, although in most cases states agree on a *modus vivendi* based on loosely defined principles of equitable utilization and good neighbourliness. Such principles are of course difficult to enforce, although they may be cited as preconditions for project aid. International funding agencies such as the World Bank refuse to fund any hydraulic projects if the water resources in question are under dispute.

The absence of multilateral or comprehensive bilateral agreements on water allocation and exploitation between Middle Eastern states is primarily linked to political mistrust in a wider sense, as well as to the relative lack of economic cooperation in the region. It is essential to remember that, although it is an emotive issue, control over water resources is only one of many bargaining tools in the political process.

Understanding the strategic significance of water in the Middle East requires consideration of the following issues. First, the concept of the water weapon itself: can it serve as a useful deterrent? An upstream state on an international river may threaten to build dams reducing flows downstream, whilst a downstream state can threaten to bomb such water diversion works. Leading political figures such as King Hussein of Jordan, President Turgut Özal of Turkey, former President Anwar Sadat of Egypt and UN Secretary-General Dr Boutros Ghali (when he was Deputy Foreign Minister of Egypt) have all referred to water as a *casus belli*,[3] but at other times these same figures have described water as an excellent focus for inter-state cooperation. Moreover, political rhetoric sometimes masks the reality of long-standing technical cooperation.

Second, although water is part of a complex system of political and economic leverages, there is very little evidence so far of actual conflict in the Middle East directly and exclusively related to the control and exploitation of water resources. At what stage would a state go to war with its neighbour to safeguard its water supply?

Hydraulic installations, such as dams, diversion tunnels, pipelines and desalination plants are vulnerable to sabotage: this was illustrated by the destruction of desalination plants in Kuwait and dams in Iraq during the Gulf War.

Shortages of water and food on a national level undoubtedly contribute to local unrest and may precipitate migration. For governments outside the region and international organizations this is arguably a greater matter for concern than localized disputes over water rights.

The principal river basin areas of the Middle East – the Jordan (and Litani), the Tigris–Euphrates and the Nile – illustrate different facets of the water crisis described above. In each of these basin areas one

6

state has demonstrably identified itself as the key player: Israel, Turkey and Egypt, respectively, operate on the assumption that their water needs and their control over water resources gives them precedence over their co-riparians.

As the issue of water resource management and allocation has crept onto the strategic agenda in the Middle East, so water-related data have become politically sensitive. As a result, no figures for water availability or consumption are undisputed or, ultimately, verifiable to a satisfactory extent. Any figures quoted in this Paper should be treated accordingly and are used to illustrate general trends.

I. THE JORDAN BASIN AND THE LITANI

The Jordan basin includes Israel and the Occupied Territories (West Bank, Gaza Strip and Golan Heights), Jordan and south-western Syria. The Litani river is also included in this region as it has often featured in hydropolitical negotiations and inter-basin transfer proposals. This region, and the Kingdom of Jordan in particular, faces the most serious water deficit in the Middle East and there is an urgent need to define a mutually acceptable framework of water management; efforts are under way as part of the Madrid peace process. Water-related tension revolves around the following issues: Israeli control over all the headwaters of the river Jordan and over portions of the Litani river in its South Lebanon Security Zone; Jordanian and Palestinian claims to 'historic' water rights on the Jordan; Syrian plans to build dams on the Yarmouk and actual dam building undermine the idea of Syrian–Jordanian joint ventures. Not enough water will be available for a joint dam with Jordan (the al-Wahda mentioned below) as Syria is in the process of capturing much of the water which was to have been stored in it for its own exclusive use. All attempts to reach agreement on water allocation between the riparian states have failed.

Control over ground-water resources in the Jordan basin is also controversial. Israel relies to a great extent on ground-water flowing from the West Bank. Restrictions on water use by the Palestinian population have been in force since occupation of the territories in 1967, while restrictions on Israeli water use were only imposed in the 1990s. In the Gaza Strip (politically rather than hydrologically part of the Jordan basin region) ground-water contamination by seawater intrusion and because of inadequate sewage facilities is leading to a grave shortage of potable (drinkable) water. The solution to the crisis lies partly in an agreement on respecting 'historic rights' claimed by the riparian states but open to differing interpretations, and partly in conservation and the development of non-conventional water resources.

On the periphery, competition for ground-water supplies between Jordan and Saudi Arabia is threatening the premature depletion of Jordan's strategic water reserve, the Disi aquifer. No bilateral settlement has yet been reached.

Hydrological context
Total water availability in the Jordan basin region is extremely limited. The Jordan river is the main axis of the system, and its total annual discharge into the Dead Sea is approximately 1,300 million cubic metres (mcm/yr). The headwaters of the Upper Jordan (550–600mcm/yr) are the Hasbani (117–140mcm/yr) river and Dan Spring (245–260mcm/yr) in Lebanon, and the Banias river (122mcm/yr) in the Golan Heights.[1] The bulk of the Upper Jordan water is stored in Lake Tiberias (also known as the Sea of Galilee or Lake Kinneret), and diverted into Israel's National Water Carrier. The Yarmouk river

(450–475mcm/yr), whose headwaters are in Syria, flows along the Syrian–Jordanian border and through the Adisiyeh triangle which borders Israel, before joining the Jordan river 10km below Lake Tiberias. Springs, ephemeral rivers and minor tributaries on the eastern and western rims of the Jordan basin contribute a further 220 and 54mcm/yr respectively.[2] The lower Jordan is saline, because of high rates of evaporation in Lake Tiberias which is partially fed by saline springs.

The figures for regional surface water use by the states in the region are disputed, especially as they form the basis of 'historic rights' claims. Nevertheless it is clear that, although Israel is, strictly speaking, a downstream state on the Jordan, its water-management policy has given it *de facto* priority usage, a situation which the Israeli government would like to maintain.

The Jordan basin region experienced low rainfall throughout the 1980s, and levels in 1990 were the lowest for 20 years; as an indication, the level of Lake Tiberias sank by four metres. The heavy rains in January–March 1992 caused widespread flooding and damage to crops mainly because of the lack of reservoir facilities.

The Litani river, the largest in Lebanon (700mcm/yr)[3], flows entirely through Lebanese territory from the Beqaa valley to the Mediterranean coast. Most of the water (432mcm) has been diverted into the Awali river for hydroelectric power (HEP) generation. However, parts of the Litani river and the Wazzani spring, which feeds the Hasbani river, lie in the Israeli-declared South Lebanon Security Zone.

National priorities

ISRAEL

Since its foundation in 1948, Israel has developed all available renewable water resources and constant overexploitation has left the country with a deficit approximately equivalent to a year's supply.[4] Efforts are being made to reduce the allocation of water to irrigated agriculture and to increase water availability from marginal sources, waste water recycling, desalination and imports. Demand for good-quality drinking water is expected to increase steadily with the continuing influx of immigrants from the former Soviet Union. The population of Israel in 1991 was 4.9 million (m), forecast to increase to 5.4m by the year 2000. Since 1989 400,000 former Soviet immigrants have settled in Israel.[5] According to a report by the State Comptroller in 1990, Israel's water deficit is principally attributable not to years of drought but rather to uncontrolled exploitation and mismanagement of resources and lack of institutional coordination.[6]

The north of the country provides 80% of Israel's water resources, whilst 65% of its agricultural land and the largest cities lie in the south. Total annual renewable freshwater resources are estimated at 1,600 mcm, 35% of which are derived from the Jordan river basin and Lake Tiberias. About 380–90mcm are diverted from Lake Tiberias to the National Water Carrier network, an integrated system to distribute water from all sources throughout the country. In addition, Israel uses approximately 70–100mcm/yr from the Yarmouk river.[7]

Ground-water supplies account for 60% of Israel's annual water supplies and these aquifers are the greatest source of concern to water planners. The principal aquifers are the coastal aquifer, with an annual safe yield estimated at 240–300mcm/yr, and the Mountain or Yarkon–Taninim aquifer which lies in the western highlands of the West Bank. The coastal aquifer has been overpumped to such a degree, particularly during the 1980s, that sea-water intrusion is widespread, large areas of the water-table have sunk below sea-level and 20% of the aquifer is damaged beyond repair. It is estimated that it will take four to five years of artificial recharge to restore water levels.[8] The safe yield of the Yarkon–Taninim aquifer is estimated at 340mcm/yr;

approximately 80% of this water, which drains naturally westwards, is used by Israeli consumers. This aquifer is considered an integral part of the Israeli network. The coastal and mountain aquifers are highly sensitive to overpumping and pollution. Smaller ground-water systems are found in Galilee, in the northern part of the West Bank (the Gilboa-Bet Shean aquifer, 140mcm/yr), and on the eastern slopes of the West Bank draining into the Jordan valley.

Water consumption in Israel was estimated at 1,750mcm in 1990, of which 1,162mcm were used for irrigation, 106mcm for industrial purposes and 482mcm for domestic supply.[9] The main problems facing the Israeli water sector are: over-use of existing stocks; lack of long-term water storage facilities (e.g., Lake Tiberias's limited capacity of 700mcm); the need to replace water distribution networks and reduce high energy costs (pumping water through the National Water Carrier accounts for 12% of Israel's total energy consumption and 40% of system operational costs). Until 1990, water consumption, particularly in agriculture, was massively subsidized; for example, in 1987 40–45% of water was sold below production costs.

Water resource management has been hampered by institutional rivalry: TAHAL (*Tichnun HaMayim le Israel*), responsible for water planning, is backed by the Jewish Agency and the Jewish National Fund. Mekorot Ltd, responsible for operation and maintenance, and the Office of the Water Commissioner are answerable to the Ministry of Agriculture, which is aware of the force of agricultural lobbies. All of these institutions have been severely criticized for wasteful and costly approaches to water management by the Office of the State Comptroller, notably in 1985 and 1990. The Water Commissioner is able to reduce water quotas to agricultural consumers but not to dictate the way in which water is used, and water prices are determined by the Ministry of Agriculture. The Ministry of Agriculture maintains that it is possible to maintain water subsidies by increasing prices without reducing water quotas.[10]

Water-management institutions have tended to adopt an *ad hoc* policy of crisis management, as illustrated by the droughts of the late 1980s and the floods of winter 1991–2. At the beginning of the 1990s Israel was facing widespread water shortages: the level of Lake Tiberias had reached an all-time low of -212.48 metres below sea level (bsl), just above the 'red line' of -213m bsl which had to be raised to -212.5m bsl. The National Water Carrier had to be shut down in January 1990 and the country faced a deficit of 400mcm.[11] In summer 1991 water allocations to farmers were cut by 50%, leading to widespread reductions in the area of irrigated cotton and orchards, but the heavy rains of winter 1991–2 flooded large areas of agricultural land in the north. The level of Lake Tiberias rose to -209.6m bsl, close to the maximum of -208.9m and enabled Mekorot Ltd to pump 1.5mcm per day into the National Water Carrier, in order to recharge the coastal aquifer. However, ultimately, the winter rains cut Israel's water deficit by only 400mcm.[12]

According to TAHAL in 1990 the transfer of water from irrigation to domestic use is part of all stated policies and plans. Agriculture played an important role during the early days of the state of Israel, when irrigation of the Negev, 'making the desert bloom', was perceived as an ideological as well as an economic priority. Israel has achieved self-sufficiency in food requirements but imports some cereals, sugar beet and animal feed.[13]

The agricultural sector has been in decline since the 1960s with a dramatic slump in the late 1980s. Agriculture accounts for only 7.6% of gross national product (GNP), and 3–4% of total export earnings. The agricultural labour force has shrunk to 5.3% of the total and the market in cotton and citrus fruits collapsed in the late 1980s. By the mid-1980s, 30% of *moshav* (smallholders' cooperative) agricultural settlements had become irrevocably uneconomic.[14] There are 430,000 hectares (ha) of land under cultivation in Israel, of which 215,000 are irrigated. Average water use per hectare has decreased by 50% with the introduction of drip and sprinkler irrigation systems. Water plans currently envisage maintaining a 37% reduction in the allocation of water to agriculture, a level of 870mcm/yr, releasing an extra 400mcm/ yr for domestic use which is expected to increase by 50mcm annually.[15] A key element of Israeli water policy for the 1990s is the gradual reduction of irrigated agriculture, accompanied by a shift in the cropping pattern away from high water-use crops such as cotton and citrus fruits. Water, if treated as an agricultural input, has so far not been cost-effective, its marginal value estimated at 35 cents per cubic metre.[16] A progressive water charging policy has been introduced, whereby farmers pay more for consuming more and are penalized for over-consumption, especially in the July–August peak period.[17] Farmers have protested strongly, however, and it has not been possible to reduce subsidized water quotas any further.[18]

Israel has already begun to utilize marginal water resources: in 1990 a total of 195mcm of recycled effluents was used, 114mcm in irrigation. The aim is to increase the range of food crops to be irrigated in this way, with the supply of waste water increasing to 240–350mcm/ yr.[19] Other plans include increasing use of ephemeral floodwaters and intermittent streams (from 40 to 80mcm/yr), and of brackish water (from 145 to 160mcm/yr by the year 2000) to irrigate salt-tolerant crops, as well as sea-water desalination. The latter is limited because of high energy costs.[20] Cloud seeding using silver iodide has been practised in the Lake Tiberias area since 1976, and target water production is 50–100mcm/yr by the turn of the century. The Israeli authorities have also considered the possibility of importing water from Turkey, either by submarine pipeline or in 700-metre long plastic bags at an estimated cost of $0.25 per cubic metre.

THE OCCUPIED TERRITORIES

The Arab population of the West Bank is entirely dependent on springs and ground-water aquifers, but uses only a small proportion of total ground-water reserves.

Total estimated annual water supply on the West Bank is 600mcm, of which 335mcm are discharged via the Mountain/Yarkon–Taninim aquifer onto the Israeli coastal plain.[21] Palestinian consumers on the West Bank use 24mcm/yr from the Yarkon–Taninim aquifer, 24mcm from aquifers flowing north into the Bet Shean valley and 59mcm/yr from aquifers on the eastern rim of the West Bank; 3mcm/yr are supplied from Israel by Mekorot Ltd.[22] The eastern aquifers are not integrated into the Israeli network and are used largely by Palestinians, although Israeli settlements in the Jordan valley abstract approximately 30mcm/yr. The Yarkon–Taninim and northern Bet Shean aquifers are essential to the Israeli water system; Israel uses 94% and 85% of their annual water yield respectively,[23] but there are no plans to connect Palestinian villages without running water to the Israeli network nor to include Palestinian agricultural areas in waste water irrigation schemes. All Israeli settlements and military outposts have piped water, whilst 70–80% of Arab villages are supplied by water tank from Mekorot Ltd.[24]

Irrigation water consumption is estimated at 80mcm/yr; industrial and domestic use accounts for 31mcm/yr.[25] The Arab population of the West Bank is approximately 1.2m (1992).[26] Demand for irrigation water is not expected to increase substantially by the year 2000, but domestic demand is set to rise to 54mcm/yr on the basis of population growth rates. Up to 45–50% of irrigation water is lost annually in piping networks.[27]

There is a wide disparity between water allocation to Israelis and Palestinians on the West Bank. In 1987 the West Bank Data Base Project forecast that, by 1990, 137mcm would be available for the Palestinian population (1m) and 100mcm for Israeli settlers (c. 100,000). According to Brigadier F. Zach, Israeli Deputy Coordinator for the Occupied Territories, West Bank Palestinians consumed 119 cubic metres per capita and Israeli settlers 354 cubic metres per capita in 1990.[28]

The issue of well-drilling is controversial: restrictions have been placed on ground-water abstraction by Palestinians: Military Order 158, 30 October 1967, Article 4 (a) stated: 'It shall not be permissible for any person to set up or to assemble or to possess or to operate a water installation unless he has obtained a licence from the area commander'. This was to prevent depletion of ground-water by unregulated drilling and overpumping. Only 34 permits for well-drilling have been issued by the Israeli authorities since 1967; all of these were for domestic rather than irrigation purposes and could not be more than 140 metres deep.[29] The Israeli authorities argued that Palestinian farmers should increase agricultural production by improving on-farm efficiency rather than by digging deeper wells. Cur-

13

rent estimates of the irrigated area of the West Bank are 3.5–6% of the cultivated area. This represents a sharp drop since 1967.[30] In addition, Palestinians have been prohibited from digging wells in the Anabta area along the western hill ridge of the West Bank, whilst Israeli settlements on both sides of the Green Line have dug approximately 17 wells for domestic and agricultural use since 1967.[31]

There are indications that ground-water abstraction by Israelis has lowered the water-table in some Arab villages and there is resentment that permission is not given to sink deeper wells. The spring in the village of al-Ouja, a widely-quoted example, has dried up repeatedly following Israeli well-drilling in the nearby settlements of Yitav and Gilgal, and the UNDP is still awaiting permission to drill a new deep well beside the old spring.[32] The water yield of wells in the villages of Tal al-Baida, Jenin, Bayt Dibs and Badila has fallen. By 1983, 12 Arab wells had dried up since the beginning of Israeli occupation.[33] There are also signs of contamination of the Yarkon–Taninim aquifer in the area of Qalqiliya and Kfar Saba by sewage effluents from the Israeli settlements of Tsofin and Alfei Menashe along the Hill Ridge.[34] Mekorot Ltd has been severely criticized by the State Comptroller for more than 25 years of overpumping of the Yarkon–Taninim aquifer; for example, in 1985 Israeli West Bank settlements exceeded their quotas by 35.5%, whereupon the State Comptroller called for compensation for Palestinian well owners.[35] Restrictions have been belatedly placed on Israeli well-digging in the West Bank by the Water Commissioner.[36]

The system of water pricing also discriminates against West Bank Palestinians. According to the West Bank Data Base Project water charges are heavily subsidized by the World Zionist Organisation:[37] settlers paid NIS (New Israeli Shekels) 0.15–0.23 (less than $0.15) per cubic metre, whilst Palestinians are charged NIS 0.70 ($0.35) by Mekorot and NIS 1–1.6 ($0.50–80) by private Arab suppliers.

Water consumption in the Golan Heights (1990 population estimate 26,000) follows a similar pattern of restrictions, following annexation by Israel in 1982. Local water resources are estimated at 20mcm/yr. Mekorot Ltd monopolizes water distribution in Golan. Israeli towns in the area, with an annual water requirement of 46mcm, are supplied with water from Lake Tiberias (16mcm) and the remainder from springs and wells and surface run-off. Water from Lake Ram, the largest body of water in the Golan, has been diverted to Israeli settlements. Run-off collection and rain-water harvesting by the Arab population have been curtailed.[38]

The pressure on water resources in the Gaza Strip (1992 population estimate 775,000)[39] is rapidly becoming intolerable, as attested by a number of economic and hydrological surveys.[40] Total water supply is estimated at 130mcm, derived principally from the coastal aquifer.[41] The safe yield of the aquifer is 65mcm/yr, but it has been overpumped by 25mcm/yr, causing large-scale sea-water intrusion and salinization at a rate of 15–20 milligram per litre (mg/l) per year.[42] As early as 1970, when ground-water abstraction was virtually unregulated, 70% of ground-water in the Gaza area exceeded salinity levels of 500 mg/l, and in some areas reached 1,500mg/l. Fifty per cent of drinking water is designated 'murky' and 23% is not drinkable at all.

Irrigation in Gaza consumes an estimated 96mcm/yr, whilst domestic consumption accounts for 13mcm[43]; industrial use is negligible at two mcm/yr. Domestic water consumption is forecast by TAHAL to increase to 37mcm/yr by the year 2000 and 57mcm by 2010, and industrial consumption to three and five mcm in the same period. The total water demand for the turn of the century is forecast at 146mcm/yr, while the population is set to reach one million. Gaza is clearly in urgent need of additional supplies from outside the area or through waste water recycling and/or desalination.

Gaza is not considered part of the Israeli water network, although Israeli settlements, in the Qatif block, are supplied by pipeline from inside the Green Line (approximately three mcm/yr).[44] Gazan water consumption, particularly for irrigation, has been restricted by Israeli policies; in 1984 estimated per capita water consumption by Gazans was 123 cubic metres, while that of Israelis was 2,326 cubic metres.[45] The immediate solution to Gaza's water deficit is curtailment of agricultural production, especially of citrus fruits, which accounts for two-thirds of irrigation water requirements and hitherto was considered to be Gaza's economic mainstay. Other options, in increasing order of cost are: rain-water harvesting, sewage treatment and reclamation, drip irrigation systems using fresh and brackish water, and desalination of brackish or sea water. If water use in irrigation can be reduced to 25–50mcm/yr, the pressure on domestic supplies will ease, but this will ultimately be determined by cost.

JORDAN

Water is one of the scarcest natural resources in Jordan; only 8.6% of the country receives more than 200mm annual rainfall. This has led to considerable anxiety among Jordanian technocrats about the country's dwindling water supplies. Jordan's population of 3.573m (1991), plus 350,000 migrant workers returning or expelled from the Gulf after the Gulf War, is expected to reach 5.67m by the year 2005.[46] Indigenous water resources cannot possibly keep pace with demand, based on current consumption trends. In addition, Jordan shares its principal water sources with its neighbours on what it regards as unfavourable terms: the Jordan and Yarmouk rivers with Syria and Israel, and ground-water reserves with Syria, Iraq and, more problematically, Saudi Arabia.

Jordan's annual water supply is approximately 800mcm/yr; 320mcm of this is from surface water (130mcm from the Yarmouk, 120 from the Jordan and the remainder from river and streams on the eastern rim of the Jordan basin); 270mcm are from renewable ground-water and 210mcm from non-renewable, the latter being Jordan's 'strategic resource', abstracted at a rate of 50mcm/yr.[47] In addition, Jordan has large reserves of fossil brackish water, up to 30,000 years old, which could yield up to 70mcm/yr.

In 1990 Jordan consumed a total of 360mcm of surface water and 383mcm of ground-water. The domestic sector accounted for 175mcm, industry for 35mcm and irrigated agriculture for 520mcm/yr, or 71.2% of the total. Consumption in the year 2005 is expected to reach 1,120mcm, of which 300 will be in the domestic sector, 70 in industry and 750mcm for irrigation. This level of consumption is clearly unthinkable on the basis of existing supplies. Jordan's ground-water is being abstracted at a rate of 170mcm beyond its safe yield, which has precipitated the decline of water tables, notably at the al-Azraq oasis, the main supplier of drinking water to Amman. The Disi aquifer, part of the strategic ground-water reserve which is shared with Saudi Arabia, could produce 100–120mcm/yr of high-quality drinking water (safe yield), to be pumped to the cities of Aqaba and eventually to Amman and Zarqa. Since 1983, Saudi Arabia has also been withdrawing water from this aquifer at Tabuk for use in agricultural projects. Pumping began at a rate of 25mcm/yr but has increased to 250mcm/yr, 50km from the Jordanian border. At this rate, the reserve will be exhausted after 25 years.[48]

Per capita annual water consumption in Jordan is one of the lowest in the world, approximately 205 cubic metres, but despite this, water demand began to outpace supply in 1987 and municipal rationing was introduced. Jordan's water deficit in summer 1991 was 210mcm and, on the basis of those trends, was set to increase to 370mcm by the turn of the century and 550mcm in 2005.

Irrigated agriculture, especially in the Jordan valley,[49] has been given priority to maximize the use of surface water before it flows into the Dead Sea. Agricultural produce from the Jordan valley, which is grown using drip irrigation and plastic greenhouses, is exported to Saudi Arabia and the Gulf states and new markets are currently being sought in Europe. Yet agriculture plays a very small role in national income generation (6.8% in 1988) or employment (7.6% of the workforce in 1988).[50] Jordan has been aiming at a degree of food security, and in 1990 food imports accounted for 19% of the total import bill, but actual rates for self-sufficiency are disappointingly low, for example 10% in wheat. The drought in summer 1991, when the storage level of dams reached an all-time low, forced the government to introduce water rationing to municipalities and to reduce the cultivated area in the Jordan valley for the 1991–2 season by one third. More extensive reductions in irrigated agriculture can only be implemented slowly, given problems of social inertia and personnel training.[51]

The problems facing water management in Jordan may be broadly summarized as: institutional competition; heavy municipal network losses (up to 55%); irrigation network losses (20% in the King Abdallah canal); inadequate storage facilities; industrial pollution and a weak water pricing policy. Given Jordan's present financial difficulties, these problems can only be addressed gradually. Jordan's current water storage capacity is 115–120mcm, while actual storage in 1990 was 65mcm. The target storage level is 387.5mcm/yr, including 220 mcm in the controversial Unity (al-Wahda) dam which may never be built.

Jordan's need for more dams and reservoirs was dramatically illustrated by the winter floods of 1991–2. Existing dams were overfilled, and flooding destroyed the bulk of Jordan's rain-fed crops in the north and 60% of crops in the Jordan valley. Plans are under way to raise existing dams and proposals for 15 new storage dams are under study, but much depends on the availability of funds. Jordan is trying to implement an International Monetary Fund (IMF) structural adjustment programme and was severely hit by the Gulf crisis (loss of remittances from expatriate workers, loss of aid from the Gulf states and loss of cut-price oil and transit trade from Iraq).

Measures are being taken to curb industrial pollution, especially in the King Talal dam area, but it has proved difficult to obtain a consensus on voluntary codes of practice. Various options are being explored for increasing the use of marginal water resources: recycled waste water currently yields 35mcm, the target is 100mcm by the year 2000 or 2010 at the latest; and the establishment of more sophisticated tertiary waste treatment plants to remove all mineral and macrobiological contamination. The whole of the Jordan valley is to be served by high-pressure drip irrigation (70,000ha are to be upgraded from surface irrigation). Ways are being sought to develop crops with lower water requirements and higher salt tolerance. Jordan eventually hopes to increase exploitation of brackish and sea water, although sea-water desalination is not economically feasible at present, given the high energy and transport network requirements. As Jordan maintained a neutral position towards Iraq during the Gulf War, it has been denied aid and low-price energy from the Gulf states.[52]

Water planners in Jordan are acutely aware of the need to educate the population in water conservation. The issue of water pricing and subsidization is controversial, however. Farmers enjoy a substantial water subsidy as a production incentive: in 1991 the cost of supplying a cubic metre of irrigation water was put at 58 fils ($0.35), but farmers only paid six fils ($0.036); this increased from three fils ($0.018) under IMF pressure, but there are no plans for any further increases.

SYRIA
Syria controls the headwaters of the Yarmouk river on which Jordan depends to such a great extent. In 1967 Syria used 50–60mcm from the upper and 20mcm from the lower Yarmouk, but the Yarmouk was not exploited to any significant extent until the mid-1970s. Since 1975 Syria has been developing the Yarmouk for irrigation and envisages a total of 25 projects to boost local economic growth. In 1991, Syria was

using 153mcm from the Yarmouk;[53] if all projects go ahead as planned, this will go up to 200mcm/yr. This is a source of great anxiety for Jordan as it will reduce the amount of water available for cereal and tobacco cultivation in the northern highlands.

LEBANON
Lebanon's importance in the regional water equation is likely to increase, but years of war have made assessments of water supply and consumption particularly difficult. Data verification is highly problematic and this has given rise to a great deal of speculation about Lebanon's water potential and, in particular, about Israeli interest in Lebanese waters.

Lebanon's water supplies are markedly seasonal and storage facilities almost non-existent. Total surface water supply is approximately 4,800mcm, including 15 permanent rivers. Of these, three are international: the Kabir (95mcm) and the Asi (also known as the Orontes, 410mcm) draining into Syria, and the Hasbani (140mcm) which flows into Israel. The largest and most exploited, relatively speaking, is the Litani river (700–900mcm estimated annual discharge).[54] Lebanon's population is estimated at 3.2m (1991), with a projected increase to 4.8m by the year 2000.[55] Total water consumption in Lebanon is approximately 900mcm: 185mcm for domestic use, 35mcm for industrial use and 670mcm for irrigation. The projected increase for the turn of the century is 1,700mcm , including 450 for domestic use, 120 for industrial purposes and 1,120 for the agricultural sector.[56] These figures for estimated water needs are significant when the question of potential water exports (inter-basin transfers) from Lebanon is considered. Lebanon's greatest potential use of water lies in hydroelectric power generation (currently only 230 megawatts). The cultivated area covers 360,000ha, of which only 87,000 are wholly or partially irrigated, mainly in the Beqaa valley and in the south. The Litani river is used principally for HEP generation but its relatively low salinity level (less than 20 mg/l) makes it an attractive source of drinking water.[57] Plans and feasibility studies were prepared in the 1950s and 1960s for a comprehensive Litani development project to develop HEP and irrigate large areas of the south to improve the standard of living of the largely Shi'i population. The HEP component was completed in 1966 with the building of a dam at Qiraoun and the Markaba diversion tunnel from the Litani river to the Awali river. Stages II and III envisaged irrigation projects along the river and the Mediterranean coast, and the construction of a dam and reservoir at Khardale.[58] The Litani Valley Authority claimed that 80% of Litani waters were still not being utilized. Plans are currently being considered to divert the Litani at its source in the Beqaa valley and to build a dam at Basri (120mcm) and at Khardale which now lies inside the South Lebanon Security Zone.[59]

Water negotiations and political tensions between the riparian states
Many attempts have been made to draw up a region-wide water management plan for the Jordan basin and a system of water allocation which is acceptable to all parties. All were undone by the long-running Arab–Israeli conflict. A perennial obstacle to negotiations has been widely differing perceptions of 'needs' and 'historic rights'. In the absence of multilateral agreements the states concerned have undertaken their own water-management projects.

The 1950s saw the most intense discussions on water allocation in a time of political tension: the spread of pan-Arab and pan-Islamic ideologies and the confrontation between radical regimes and monarchies. Most of the problems discussed in the 1950s are still on the negotiating agenda. In the 1950s Israel's priorities were the greening of the Negev desert and the settlement of new immigrants, a matter of 'national economic importance',[60] and one which also strengthened the immigrants' psychological attachment to the land of Israel. Israel's Arab neighbours, in particular Jordan, claimed that the Jordan basin waters were needed primarily for the resettlement of Palestinian refugees, especially the 800,000 living on both banks of the Jordan. Negotiations centred around surface waters.

The 1944 Lowdermilk plan, elaborated in the more technical Hays-Savage plan of 1948, was backed by the World Zionist Organisation. It proposed: using Jordan and Litani river waters to irrigate the Negev in Israel; the storage of Yarmouk floodwaters in Lake Tiberias; and the construction of a canal from the Mediterranean coast to the Dead Sea. The 1951 Sir Murdoch MacDonald report also advocated the diversion of the Yarmouk river into Lake Tiberias. The Bunger-UNRWA plan of 1952 was more appealing to Jordan and Syria: it proposed the construction of a dam on the Yarmouk at Maqarin on the Syrian–Jordanian border and a dam at Adisiyeh to divert Yarmouk waters into the Jordan valley along the East Ghor canal; it advised against storage in Lake Tiberias.[61] In June 1953 Syria and Jordan concluded a water-sharing agreement for the Yarmouk, to which Israel objected, whilst pursuing its own water diversion plan on the Upper Jordan at Jisr Banat Yaqub. The dispute was internationalized when Syria brought the case to the United Nations Security Council in September 1953[62] and prompted attempts at mediation by the US.

The most sustained efforts at reaching a multilateral accord were made between 1953 and 1955 by US Ambassador Eric Johnston. The Johnston Plan, based on an idea originally elaborated by the US Tennessee Valley Authority, would establish a system of water quotas for the riparian states using Lake Tiberias as the principal storage reservoir. Storage dams would also be built on the Hasbani, Dan and Banias to irrigate Galilee in northern Israel, and at Maqarin and Adisiyeh to serve the Jordan valley. Most controversially, the implementation of the Plan was to be supervised by a loosely defined international commission. The final version of the plan, known as the

Revised Unified Plan of October 1955, proposed the following allocations from the Jordan, Yarmouk, Hasbani, Banias and side wadis in the Jordan valley. These quotas and their basis were the object of intense negotiation.

Table: Water Allocations under the Revised Unified Plan (mcm)

	Total	Jordan	Yarmouk	Other
Jordan	720	100	377	243
Israel	375–400*	375	25	
Syria	132	22	90	20
Lebanon	35			35
Total	1,287			

Sources: T. Naff and R. Matson, *Water in the Middle East: Conflict or Cooperation?* (Boulder, CO: Westview Press, 1985); S.N. Saliba, *The Jordan River Dispute* (The Hague: Martinus Nijhoff, 1968); A. Soffer and N. Kliot, 'The Water Resources of the Jordan Catchment: Management Options', in British Society for Middle East Studies (BRISMES), *Annual Conference Proceedings, 1991*, pp. 205–10.

Note:
* Israel was to receive 'residual' flows from the Jordan river.

Johnston's aim was that the division of waters should be 'equitable, economic and efficient'. The Plan was accepted by the technical teams representing the negotiating parties, but not ratified by either the Israeli cabinet or the Arab League Council, and, amidst press hysteria and public outcry, it was subsequently thrown out altogether by the Arab governments concerned. Its rejection was entirely on political grounds: Lebanon, Syria and Jordan were reluctant to enter into a cooperative agreement with a state which they did not recognize. In addition, they were anxious that the US had offered Israel guarantees on border security in return for acquiescence regarding water allocation to Jordan.[63] The emphasis on water allocation was seen in the Lebanese press as a means of diverting attention from the problem of Palestinian refugees; nor could the Arab states be pressurized as easily as Israel with US financial aid.[64] In the age of pan-Arabism, when enmity of Israel was the principal unifying factor among the Arab states, no Arab leader could be seen to be cooperating openly with the enemy. Nor did the Johnston Plan, which did not include the Litani river, ultimately appeal to the Israelis, who felt that their own water diversion plans would bring much higher yields.

Although the Johnston Plan was never implemented, the quotas have provided a working arrangement for the riparian states. At the time, the Israeli government was more enthused by the Cotton Plan (February 1954), which included the Litani river and raised Israel's share of regional waters to 1,290mcm (out of 2,345.7mcm).[65] The Arab

Technical Committee put forward a plan in March 1954 giving Jordan a much higher allocation of 975mcm, whilst Jordan commissioned the Baker-Harza Plan in 1955 for a storage dam on the Yarmouk basin and the irrigation of up to 46,000ha in the Jordan valley. Arab-sponsored plans rejected the idea of transferring water from the Litani.

From the late 1950s onwards the states of the Jordan basin pressed on with individual hydraulic projects: Jordan pursued a major irrigation project in the Jordan valley fed by the East Ghor (now King Abdallah) canal (1957), whilst Israel built the National Water Carrier (completed 1964). Both states received US aid. The failure of regional negotiations contributed to inter-state tension. The 1964–5 Arab Headwaters Diversion Plan, instigated by President Nasser of Egypt and carried out by Syria to divert the waters of the Banias and Hasbani rivers into the Yarmouk and thus thwart Israel's own diversion works by reducing the Upper Jordan flow by up to 35%, was regarded as provocative by Israel. The installations were bombed by Israel in April 1967, two months before the Six-Day War. The project would have given the Arab states less water than they could have expected under the Johnston Plan, but it was seen by Israel to symbolize the growing regional influence of Egypt and Syria, and was consequently regarded as dangerous.[66]

In the period 1967–70 the Israeli army repeatedly shelled the East Ghor (now known as the King Abdallah) canal and the Jordan valley in retaliation for Palestine Liberation Organisation (PLO) incursions into Israel from bases in Jordan. This was not a dispute over water supply: water installations were regarded as strategic targets.[67]

More recent developments in regional water planning have not offered any promising long-term solutions either. In the early 1970s the Jordanian government revived the idea of a storage dam at Maqarin and a diversion dam at Adisiyeh as part of a general programme to extend and rehabilitate cultivation in the Jordan valley. The US was approached for aid, but the scheme did not go ahead as Jordan required the cooperation of Syria and Israel. In the 1980s Jordan became anxious about the amount of water used in Syrian projects on the Yarmouk and the impact this would have on its future water supply from the river. In July 1987 Syria and Jordan signed an agreement to build the Unity (al-Wahda) dam at Maqarin to store 225mcm under terms very favourable to Syria. Syria was to receive 75% of the electricity generated while Jordan bore the costs of construction, receiving 180mcm of water in return. Jordan's application for funds from the World Bank ($US 300m) was rejected because Israel, as co-riparian, vetoed the project saying it would adversely affect Israel's use of 15% of Yarmouk waters. At the time of writing, Israel had not made a formal statement of non-objection to the project, and indeed had threatened to bomb the Unity/Maqarin dam if it were ever built. However, some cooperation regarding water does exist between Israel and Jordan: in 1979–80 the two states negotiated a confidential agreement whereby Israel agreed to use only 25mcm of Yarmouk flows in winter in return for assurances regarding higher summer flows. Sandbags were placed at the entrance to the King Abdallah canal to facilitate the diversion of winter Yarmouk flows into the Jordan valley. The entrance to the canal is also regularly cleared of sandbars, natural or man-made, by Israeli and Jordanian engineers.

In 1980 Israeli engineers submitted a proposal for the construction of a canal from the Mediterranean to the Dead Sea to generate HEP, but it was opposed by Jordan on the grounds that raising the level of the Dead Sea would flood tourist facilities, roads and destroy potash production installations.[68] Yet these objections were ultimately political rather than economic: Jordan subsequently submitted an alternative proposal for a canal to the Dead Sea, from the Red Sea at Aqaba.[69] However, a surprising degree of bilateral cooperation does exist: for instance, the drip irrigation systems used in the Jordan valley are purchased via Israel.

Prospects for conflict and cooperation
It is questionable whether the basin-wide quota-based approach to water management is relevant or practicable in the 1990s. This does not necessarily imply inevitable water wars or chronic instability. Arguably, independent economic development in border regions such as the Jordan valley and the Yarmouk basin in Syria suggests a move away from more warlike postures.[70] A measure of unofficial cooperation does exist, despite the riparian states' differing perceptions of water needs at present. The question today is whether the long-term solution to the deepening water crisis is technical, through the development of marginal resources and increasing the total amount of water available in the area, or politico-legal, based on a recognition of 'historic rights' or at least the principle of water-sharing. In either case the most salient issue is control over the sources of supply. Water is a pivotal issue at the talks in Madrid on the Middle East peace process. Multilateral discussions have taken place between Israeli, Jordanian and Palestinian delegates in Moscow, Vienna and Washington in parallel to bilateral talks on territory and sovereignty and on administrative arrangements for the Palestinians. Yet little substantive progress has been made. Syria and Lebanon have stated that no discussions on any of the multilateral issues, including arms control, refugees, economic development and environmental protection, have any value unless Israel withdraws from occupied Arab land.

Israel regards its water needs as paramount and control over the sources of the Jordan river and key aquifers as a minimum security requirement.[71] Israeli security perceptions remain strongly territorial, and while policy-makers recognize the serious water deficit in Jordan and Gaza and advocate international cooperative water management to ensure quality controls, they also stress that Israel's 'rightful shares' must be preserved. The quota system advocated in the Johnston Plan is seen as anachronistic: since Israeli occupation of the West Bank, the movement of settlers into the West Bank and the influx of Palestinians into Jordan, these quotas would in any case have to be modified. Israel denies that it has been 'stealing' water from its neighbours. At the Moscow multilateral peace negotiations in January 1992, the Israeli Water Commissioner stated that Israel favours the cooperative use of unused resources, the production of new water by building desalination plants and coordination of efforts to control pollution.

This sidesteps more fundamental issues, however. Israeli control of the Yarkon–Taninim and Bet Shean aquifers on the West Bank is a key factor in its reluctance to relinquish the West Bank in a 'land-for-peace' deal. Palestinian control over these aquifers, it is feared, would mean inadequate abstraction monitoring, unregulated well-drilling, pumping and contamination by toxic waste.

The Israeli Ministry of Agriculture issued a statement in August 1990 announcing that: 'it is difficult to conceive of any political solution consistent with Israel's survival that does not involve complete continued Israeli control of the [West Bank]'s water and sewerage systems, and of the associated infrastructure...'[72] In addition, water demand on the West Bank would increase if diaspora Palestinians returned to a newly-created Palestinian state. It has been suggested that, if such a state is ever established, Israel should retain control over the 2–6-km wide hill ridge in the Anabta area. Any agreement on water must include a proviso that Israel maintains its current level of utilization of the Mountain/Yarkon–Taninim aquifer. If the Golan Heights were to be returned to Syria, this could jeopardize Israel's access to the Banias river. Israel advocates proposals to supply the Palestinians on the West Bank and in Gaza with water from Egypt, Lebanon or Turkey.[73] The Israeli government refuses to negotiate with the Palestinians on water rights, except on municipal supplies, until the third year of a five-year interim administration period, the objective of the Madrid peace process. The former Israeli Water Commissioner, Dan Zaslavsky, recently summarized the official position: 'Israel does not want to become dependent for water on any neighbouring country, even in peacetime'.[74]

Rather than continue to reshuffle meagre existing resources, Israeli policy-makers back projects which will increase the overall water supply. Two main approaches have been investigated: importing water from outside the basin, and building Arab–Israeli joint venture desalination plants on the Mediterranean coast. Proposals for out-of-basin transfers include: storing Litani waters in Lake Tiberias or in a dam on the Yarmouk to supply Jordan and the West Bank; a submarine pipeline from Turkey; a pipeline from the Ceyhan and Seyhan rivers in Turkey to supply Syria, Jordan and the West Bank; importing Litani water to Israel in exchange for electricity; and, finally, importing Nile water to Gaza via a Sinai canal. Jordan and the Palestinians, it is implied, should forgo claims to the Yarmouk.

The water deficit in the Gaza Strip could be solved if it had access to 1% of the annual flow of the Nile (84km^3) according to another plan. This was first proposed by Theodor Herzl in 1903 as part of a plan to settle Jews in Sinai, and was later revived and supported by President Anwar Sadat of Egypt in 1978–9. Nile waters could, at a later stage, be conveyed to the Negev and sold to Israel. The proposal was widely opposed in Egypt and by Ethiopia which supplies 86% of Nile water. It is not a practical option at present as Egypt is planning to pipe 3km^3 of Nile waters annually through the El-Salaam canal to serve agricultural and other development projects in northern Sinai.

The present Israeli administration and leading water planners are strongly in favour of desalination plants on the Mediterranean coast, near Gaza, Hadera, Ashdod and Haifa, and running costs are estimated as low as $0.75–0.80 per cubic metre (although this is disputed and TAHAL claims the figure is closer to $2 per cubic metre). This new water could be exported to the Occupied Territories and to Jordan, but most of the plants would obviously be in Israeli-controlled territory. At the multilateral discussions on water in Vienna from 13 to 14 May 1992 Israeli representatives emphasized Israel's opposition to reapportioning existing water supplies.

Israel's Arab negotiating partners, in particular Jordan and the Palestinians, claim legal entitlement to various portions of the Jordan system waters now used by Israel. The Palestinian position is that a 'land-for-peace' arrangement and the establishment of a Palestinian administration in the West Bank and Gaza Strip is a precondition for any negotiations on water. The Palestinians insist that the principal problem is authority over indigenous water resources, and call for the restoration of 'historic rights' and a minimum quota of 200mcm/yr to be granted retrospectively.[75] Only after 'historic rights' are restored can Israelis and Palestinians enter into negotiations on limited regional cooperation, storage dams on the Yarmouk or desalination plants. There is resentment that the Johnston Plan and others in the 1950s did not regard the Palestinians as a distinct political entity. The economy of a putative Palestinian state would rely, in the early stages, on agriculture and agro-industry, requiring an expansion in the irrigated area. Existing water supplies are inadequate. Ironically, a re-established Palestine would be surrounded by states seeking to reduce their irrigated areas.

Initially, the Palestinians seek access to hydrological data denied to them since the imposition of Military Order 92 (15 August 1967). On 14 May 1992 at the Vienna multilateral talks on water, Palestinians, Jordanians and Israelis agreed in principle to cooperate on the exchange of data.

The Jordanian position is that water allocation must be user-related, and that negotiations should seek to 'move from a position of disparity to equitable utilisation of water'.[76] Domestically, the most important task is to make water use more efficient and to increase the yield from marginal sources. Jordan is pressing for what it considers to be a more equitable share of Jordan river waters and for a more satisfactory working arrangement with Syria; it is widely felt that Jordan has been left with the water residue of its neighbours over whom it has minimal leverage.

In the multilateral negotiations on water, Jordan expects clear concessions from Israel on the principle of water-sharing. Jordan has prepared an agenda which advocates water-saving measures and cooperation on desalination projects, for example, but there can be no progress without political gestures. Meanwhile, Jordan has still not resolved the problem of water-sharing with Syria or Saudi Arabia. It is doubtful whether the Unity dam project will ever go ahead, given the scale of Syria's own utilization of Yarmouk waters. As an indication of this, Jordan has put its efforts into the building of a new national storage dam (55mcm) at Karameh. There are few prospects at present of a Jordanian–Saudi agreement on the Disi aquifer: Jordanian officials claim that they have spent at least five years trying to persuade the Saudi government to agree to a bilateral accord.

Syria and Lebanon (the latter's foreign and economic policies are in effect monitored by Syria under the May 1991 Treaty of Brotherhood, Cooperation and Coordination), have been boycotting the Moscow and Vienna sessions on water. The Syrian view is that no negotiations with Israel on water are possible until Israel withdraws from occupied Arab lands, particularly the Golan Heights. As further preconditions for negotiations, Syria insists that there should be an internationally-acceptable delimitation of its border with Israel, and that Palestinian water rights should be restored and hydrological data exchanged. Syria claims that Jordan's water deficit will be solved by the Unity dam, and that the project is being undermined by Israeli vetoes rather than its own development activities.

Lebanon is strongly opposed to any proposals to export Litani waters. All Zionist and Israeli-backed plans for Jordan basin water management have included the Litani in the river system. As early as 1920, during Anglo-French discussions on the boundaries of Mandate Palestine, Chaim Weizmann wrote to the then British Foreign Secretary, Lord Curzon:

> Your Lordship realises the enormous importance of the Litani to Palestine. Even if the whole of the Jordan and the Yarmouk are included in Palestine it has insufficient water for its needs. . . The irrigation of upper Galilee and the power necessary for even a limited industrial life must come from the Litani. . . If Palestine were cut off from the Litani, Upper Jordan and the Yarmouk she could not be economically independent.[77]

In 1982, after the second Israeli invasion of Lebanon, 'Operation Peace for Galilee', Israeli forces established the front line of their Security Zone along the Litani river and examined hydrological data belonging to the Litani River Authority. A number of reports have alleged that Israeli engineers drew up plans to divert Litani waters at the Khardale bridge into the Jordan valley via the Hasbani river. This would allow Israel to withdraw at least 100mcm/yr from the Litani.[78] As such a small quantity of water would have only a limited impact on Israel's water budget, it is barely worth the expense of engineering works. In order to withdraw more substantial amounts of water from the Litani, Israel would have to destroy the Qiraoun reservoir and the Markaba tunnel to prevent the diversion into the Awali river. No evidence for Israeli water diversions has been produced. Lebanon insists that its water supplies are non-negotiable and hydrologists maintain that there are no exportable surpluses. Israel will, however, insist on maintaining control over the Hasbani river and Dan spring in the event of withdrawal from south Lebanon.

Despite differing needs and security perceptions by the riparian states there is no indication that the water crisis in the Jordan basin will be resolved by military action. It has been suggested that a limited war costing an estimated $1bn per day with destruction of water installations could not solve long-term problems of supply, and the negative economic and infrastructural impacts would greatly outweigh those of desalination plants.[79]

Efforts are being made to conserve water on a national level and this process will have to intensify; much depends on the management of the agricultural sector, but political sensibilities also have to be taken into account. On an international level the agreement on the principle of information exchange is significant, although the extent to which it can be implemented remains to be seen. Ad hoc consultation and tacit cooperation on water management are likely to persist and offset any belligerent rhetoric. Ultimately, unless there are substantive agreements under the Madrid peace process on wider issues of sovereignty and territory, enthusiasm for cooperation on technical projects will continue to be limited.

II. THE TIGRIS–EUPHRATES BASIN REGION

The Tigris–Euphrates basin region includes Turkey, Syria, Iraq and Iran. Turkey, Syria and Iraq all plan to use the waters of the Euphrates and Tigris and their tributaries for irrigation and have invested in large-scale dam projects, the largest of which is Turkey's South-East Anatolia Project (GAP – *Güneydogu Anadolu Projesi*). Turkey, as the upstream state on the Tigris and Euphrates, is exercising what its government interprets as its sovereign right to exploit water in its territory, a right which its downstream neighbours strenuously dispute. If all projects under the GAP umbrella go ahead as planned the flow of the Euphrates and eventually the Tigris could be substantially reduced and the filling of Turkish reservoirs will cause several interruptions in river flow. Although the final extent of the project and the completion date are not known, GAP will inevitably compete with continuing Syrian and Iraqi plans to increase their irrigated agricultural areas.

The other main area of controversy is the Asi (Orontes) river: Syria is the *de facto* upstream state and its irrigation schemes have virtually halted the flow of the river into Turkey's Hatay province, an area which is claimed by Syria.

Water is only one of the factors souring relations between Turkey, Syria and Iraq, states traditionally competing for regional leadership. There is no doubt that some of the hydrological consequences of GAP can only add to regional tensions, but the underlying causes of instability are Kurdish nationalism and border security, and the support for regime opponents by neighbouring states.

There are significant Kurdish minorities in Turkey, Syria, Iraq and Iran: Kurds account for 19% of the population in Turkey, and 23% in Iraq.[1] They are represented by a number of political parties with military wings, notably the PKK (Kurdish Workers' Party) in Turkey, and the KDP (Kurdish Democratic Party) and the PUK (Patriotic Union of Kurdistan) in Iraq. At various times these parties have been backed by Turkey, Syria, Iraq and Iran as a means of destabilizing each other politically. The question of Syrian support for PKK *peshmerga*, or guerrillas, has overshadowed Turkish–Syrian relations during the 1980s. In response to Iraqi refusals to reach an acceptable solution to the demarcation of the Shatt al-Arab boundary river, Iran gave material support to the KDP during the Kurdish rebellion in northern Iraq in the mid-1970s until the Iran–Iraq Algiers agreement of 1975. In the late 1980s Turkey launched a number of raids against PKK bases in northern Iraq in response to incursions into south-east Anatolia. Border security and Kurdish nationalism preoccupy the states in the region to a greater extent than concern over the consequences of Turkey's GAP. These overarching political issues have coloured approaches to water policy; the Tigris–Euphrates basin states have directed their energies into decrying the unreasonable actions of

Tigris and Euphrates basin

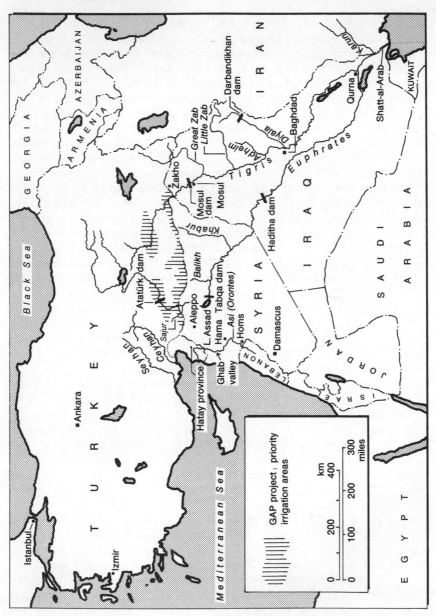

GAP project : priority irrigation areas

their neighbours rather than into solving the problem of domestic water distribution.

Hydrological context
The headwaters of the Tigris and Euphrates rivers and the main tributaries of the Euphrates are in Turkey. Natural river flows are highly variable. The average annual discharge of the Euphrates at the Turkish–Syrian border is 30.377km^3 and 31.8km^3 at Hit in Iraq, but has varied from 16–50km^3. The average annual discharge of the Tigris at the Turkish border is 16.8km^3, 18.5 km^3 at Mosul. Tributaries in Iraq add a further 26.7km^3. Over 98% of Euphrates flow, including the main tributaries of the Khabur, Sajur and Balikh rivers, originates in Turkey, although Turkey accounts for only 28% of the basin area.[2] Turkey also contributes 45% of the flow of the Tigris. The remaining Tigris flow is contributed by tributaries in Iraq whose headwaters lie in Iran: the Adheim, the Greater and Lesser Zab and the Diyala rivers. The Tigris and Euphrates converge at Qurna in Iraq and are joined by the Karun river (15.5km^3/yr) which rises in Iran; the combined rivers, known as the Shatt al-Arab (43.8km^3/yr) drain into the Gulf. Water quality declines downstream, from less than 250mg/l in Turkey to over 600mg/l in lower Iraq and 5,000mg/l south of Basra.

The Asi (Orontes) river rises in Lebanon and flows through Syria into the Hatay region of Turkey. Its discharge at the Lebanese–Syrian border is estimated at 410mcm, and 1,200mcm at the Syrian–Turkish border. Ninety percent of the average annual discharge of the Asi is used by Syria.

National priorities
TURKEY
Turkey has relatively abundant water resources, but these are unevenly distributed and under-utilized. Average annual rainfall in Turkey is 642mm and the country has 26 major river basins. Total surface water supply is 185 cubic kilometres/year, of which only 95km^3 can be exploited. The Tigris and the Euphrates account for one-third of Turkey's surface water supply.[3] Annual ground-water potential in the Tigris–Euphrates basin area is estimated at 1.526km.[4]

Although agriculture accounts for the bulk of water consumption in Turkey (32km^3), and agricultural development of south-east Anatolia has become an economic priority, one of the more serious long-term problems facing water planners is how to supply rapidly growing urban populations. The country's population was 56.5m in 1990 and, with annual average growth rates of 2.2%, is set to rise to 70m by the year 2000. Fifty-nine percent of the population already lives in cities. According to the 1990 Census, the urban population increased by 43.1% in the period 1985–90. Demand for water is growing rapidly in the metropolitan areas of Istanbul, Ankara and Izmir, and along the Aegean and Mediterranean coasts as a result of tourist development.

These cities will have to be supplied from rivers farther and farther afield: Ankara, for example, by the Kizindirmak and Sakaria rivers which are 90km away.[5]

Turkey looks on its rivers as sources of water for irrigation and also for HEP. Turkey is largely self-sufficient in food production, and is a leading regional exporter of fruit and vegetables to the Middle East and Europe. The country's agricultural potential has not yet been fully exploited: out of 28m ha of arable land, only 3.3m have been developed for irrigation; 8.5m are considered economically irrigable, depending on the way in which water is costed and on the pace of agricultural liberalization. The agricultural sector in western Turkey became more mechanized during the 1980s. Structural reforms of the agricultural sector are being implemented, subsidies on wheat production are being reduced, but skewed land tenure – particularly the concentration of large areas of land in the hands of a small number of very powerful landowners or *agas* – remains a problem, especially in the south-east. Agriculture contributes 18.5% of Turkey's GDP and employs 50% of the workforce.

Turkey's water projects are largely motivated by a quest for cheaper, domestically-produced energy. Turkey imports 50% of its annual energy requirements and 25% of electricity production depends on imported fuel; its oil bill in 1990 was $3.5bn.[6] If Turkey is to achieve its stated target of 5% annual economic growth, electricity production needs to double every 10–15 years. The Euphrates and Tigris account for 40% of HEP potential and are expected to supply 25% of electricity in Turkey if the GAP project is fully implemented. HEP-generating dams have been built on the Euphrates river at Keban in 1974 (1,360MW installed capacity) and at Karakaya in 1989 (1,800MW).

By far the most ambitious development scheme in Turkey at present is the South-East Anatolia Project which is designed to harness the waters of the Tigris and the Euphrates rivers for HEP generation and irrigation. GAP has caused great anxiety to Turkey's downstream neighbours, Syria and Iraq, who fear that reduced river flows will damage their own agricultural and energy projects. The hydropolitical implications of GAP appear to pose a threat to regional stability; the building of the Atatürk dam was widely portrayed as a belligerent act in the Arab media, but an examination of the economic and technical aspects of GAP puts such images in perspective.

It is important to remember that GAP is above all a domestic project to develop the relatively impoverished region of south-east Anatolia. Its aim is to develop agriculture and agro-industrial production for export and to raise the standard of living of the Kurdish population in the area. Agricultural production is a priority as the designated growth poles are based on agro-industry, and Turkey plans to export agricultural produce to the Middle East and the Commonwealth of Independent States, especially the emerging states of Central Asia. GAP was conceived as the economic answer to Kurdish demands for self-determination and not as a means of international political leverage, although it has been perceived as such to some extent by Syria and Iraq.

The project area covers the provinces of Gaziantep, Diyarbakir, Sanliurfa, Mardin, Adiyaman and Siirt. It does not cover the whole of the Kurdish region, which includes the provinces of Van and Hakkari for topographical reasons. The regional population accounts for 9% of the national total with net emigration trends. Economic development has lagged behind that of western Turkey: the GAP region is character-ized by higher population growth rates, lower *per capita* GDP and *per capita* income only 40% of the national average of $1,600 (1990). GAP aims to create at least 90,000 public sector jobs in the region and estab-lish agricultural and industrial growth poles to attract Western inves-tors. It hopes to turn the area into a regional bread-basket: 'to mobilise regional resources, to eradicate regional disparities, to enhance pro-ductivity, to create employment opportunities, to raise income levels, to develop urban centres and to ensure economic growth and social stability in the region'.[7] Whether such aims or the expectations of the project's local beneficiaries are ever likely to be realized is debatable.

The parameters are certainly grandiose. Spending has totalled $9bn since 1981. If all projects are completed, officials estimate the total costs will be $32bn. GAP consists of 13 main projects: seven on the Euphrates and six on the Tigris: 21 dams in total and 19 HEP generating stations. The centrepiece is the Atatürk dam (started in 1983) on the Euphrates with a total storage capacity of 48.7km^3, an installed electricity-generating capacity of 2,400MW and a generating target of 27bn kilowatt-hour per year. The dam will also regulate Euphrates flows. The first turbines became operational when the reservoir volume reached 29km^3 in July 1992. Other dams currently under construction are at Birecik (Euphrates, late 1992–3) and Ilisi (Tigris, 1996–2001).[8]

Over 1.6m ha, (1.08m on the Euphrates and 600,000ha on the Tigris) are scheduled for irrigation, although these figures are con-stantly being revised. Only 114,000ha are currently irrigated in the area, using mostly ground-water. On the Urfa and Harran plains 256,000ha have been designated priority irrigation areas and will be supplied from the Atatürk dam via the twin Urfa tunnels. The first 40,000ha will be supplied in 1993. The project has been designed for surface (flood) irrigation largely in open channels, with some localized pilot sprinkler systems, and is therefore highly water-consuming.

Completion dates for these projects are difficult to estimate, given various technical and, more importantly, financial constraints. If all developments go ahead as planned, the flow of the Euphrates into Syria will be reduced by up to 11km^3 (assuming one hectare of land uses 10,000m^3 of water per yr) and that of the Tigris by up to six km^3/ yr. Syria and Iraq are also concerned about deterioration in water quality; some irrigation water will flow back into the rivers and these are likely to contain higher levels of pesticides, fertilisers and salts.

These figures depend, however, on the overall progress of GAP, which faces a number of constraints.

The first obstacle is funding: GAP is financed almost entirely from Turkish sources. The government was refused aid from the World Bank on the grounds that there was no agreement on water rights between the riparian states. GAP accounts for 6–9% of the national budget, and spending (estimated at $1.5m per day) has contributed to Turkey's annual rate of inflation of 70%. International investment in the area has been sluggish to say the least: the region is considered unstable because of Kurdish separatist activities and infrastructural facilities are lacking.

The local impact of GAP is controversial. Some would argue that it has raised nothing but expectations. There has been more emphasis on dam-building than on the development of roads, educational and training and agricultural extension facilities. Farmers do not have access to adequate credit facilities, nor have they received sufficient training in irrigation techniques. Salinization and waterlogging of the soil – the consequences of over-irrigation – are already in evidence in the GAP area. Planners point out that water-saving methods are being introduced on main canals. At farm level, however, it is hard to implement a water-pricing policy on a volume basis (it is currently based on the size of the irrigated area), and water meters have been destroyed.[9] The problem of land ownership is in urgent need of attention in a region where 8% of farmers possess 50% of the land. In addition, the flooding of the Atatürk dam reservoir displaced approximately 70,000 people from 117 villages in the area; most of them invested their compensation money not in agricultural land but in houses in Sanliurfa. In sum, supplying the water itself is the easiest stage in the development process.

SYRIA
Whilst Turkish exploitation of the Euphrates river is alarming because it is relatively recent, the Syrian experience is long and troubled. Problems have ranged from deterioration in soil quality to clashes of interest between farmers and bureaucrats, and projects have fallen far short of their targets.

Total surface water resources in Syria, excluding the Euphrates river, are $9.94km^3/yr$.[10] The natural flow of the Euphrates at Jarablous is $28km^3$. Under a bilateral agreement with Turkey in 1987 Syria receives $15.75km^3/yr$ from the Euphrates (500 cubic metres per second) and according to a bilateral agreement with Iraq in 1990, $6.6km^3$ of this (42%) is used in Syria and the remaining $9km^3$ are allowed to flow into Iraq. The annual renewable ground-water supply is approximately $5.1km^3/yr$. Rainfall in the country varies from less than 100mm/yr in the desert steppe (Badia) to 1,300mm/yr on the coast.

Irrigated agriculture accounts for the bulk of water consumption: $8.8km^3/yr$ in 1989/90, whilst the domestic and industrial sectors used

820mcm and 1,000mcm/yr respectively. The expansion of irrigation and domestic food production continues to be viewed as an economic priority and the Euphrates region is the main development target area. Three dams have already been built on the Euphrates: the Tabqa dam (completed in 1975, with 14.2km³ storage capacity and 860-MW installed HEP capacity), the al-Baath regulatory dam and the Tishreen HEP dam (completed in 1991 with 1.9km³/yr storage and 630-MW installed capacity).

The Tabqa dam was to be the centrepiece of the Euphrates valley project to irrigate 640,000ha. However, the schemes in the Tabqa area were adversely affected by high gypsum levels in the soil and by salinization caused by overpumping and by collapse of canals due to seepage (5m³/sec). The actual area to have been reclaimed is approximately 240,000ha. The total irrigated area in Syria is officially put at 863,308ha (500,000 in 1975), of which 309,000ha are on the Euphrates and 207,844ha are on the Tigris and the Khabur.[11] Syria plans to press ahead with land reclamation targets to increase the irrigated area to 1.4m ha by 2010, which, in the light of expected Turkish utilization of the Euphrates as well as existing management difficulties seems somewhat unrealistic. 11.6km³ would be required from the Tigris and Euphrates. Syria will require a total of 8.3km³ from the Euphrates: 7.6km³ for irrigation, 500mcm for industry and 128mcm for drinking water.[12]

In addition, Syria's five-year plan calls for expansion of the irrigated areas on the Khabur, Sajur and Balikh rivers, on the Tigris in the Hassaka region and on the Asi river. Syria has been using the Asi river since 1961 for irrigated agriculture in the Ghab valley. The Rustam (250mcm) and Hilfaya-Mehardeh (65mcm) dams also provide electricity for the cities of Homs and Hama. Two additional dams, the Ziezoun and Kastoun (total 98mcm), are planned to regulate the erratic flow of the Asi; this would reduce the flow into Turkey to 25mcm/yr. Under the terms of the 1972 Syrian–Lebanese agreement, Lebanon was allocated 80mcm of Asi waters. Approximately 230,000ha are irrigated by the Asi and 27,000 by the Yarmouk. Syria and Lebanon have been discussing the feasibility of joint development projects on the Asi.

Irrigation and HEP projects have encountered technical and social problems: the Soviet design of the Tabqa dam, which produces 60% of the country's electricity, is not appropriate for local topography, hence low flows in summer substantially reduce power generation. This leads to power cuts in the major cities, especially Aleppo and Damascus. Irrigation is seen as a means of increasing productivity: irrigated areas account for only 12.8% of cultivated land, but 50% of the value of agricultural production. The predominant use of surface irrigation methods, however, means that 50–55% of water is lost in the network. Under the seventh five-year plan (1990–4), priority has been given to improving irrigation efficiency to at least 76%. A one percent increase in water-delivery efficiency would save 127mcm/yr. Seventy-five percent of spending in the agricultural sector (11% of the plan budget, the second highest allocation after defence) has been allocated to improving on-farm irrigation efficiency.[13] Land tenure is another long-standing problem, especially fragmentation and resistance to cooperatives.[14]

In 1990 agricultural production accounted for 28% of GDP and employed 25% of the workforce. However, Syrian agriculture is becoming more marginal to the economy, and cotton, once Syria's main export earner, is being superseded by oil. In 1989 oil accounted for 27% of export earnings by value.[15] Officials realize that land reclamation targets are very ambitious and that total food security can never be achieved, but insist that relative food security in staple crops is essential, regardless of economic viability.

The Syrian economy is undergoing many transformations: it has long been dominated by a heavy military budget which the Syrian troop presence in Lebanon continues to drain. In the 1970s and 1980s Syria was dependent on aid from Arab states, by virtue of its position as a front-line state against Israel (this aid accounted for 55% of foreign-exchange receipts). Syria was promised further grants by the Arab Gulf states and the EC in return for supporting the anti-Iraq coalition during the Gulf War. Since the end of that war, economic liberalization and the search for Western investment are now very much on the agenda. Oil is the expanding sector of the economy: current production is 500,000 barrels/day and revenues are set to increase. Hence, given the obvious difficulties facing the agricultural sector and the amount of basic infrastructural repairs which need to be undertaken, the viability of land reclamation targets is questionable. When assessing Syria's likely water requirements from the Euphrates and the extent to which its plans might be jeopardized by events upstream these economic factors must be taken into account.

IRAQ
Average rainfall in Iraq is 800mm/yr, ranging from less than 150mm in the south-western desert to over 1,892mm/yr in the mountains of the north-east. Total surface water resources are approximately 80km^3/yr: 31km^3 from the Euphrates and almost 50km^3 from the Tigris. Iraq's main problem is water quality rather than quantity. It has relatively abundant water resources, but serious problems with water management and soil salinity have dogged irrigation projects throughout the history of Mesopotamia. The variable flow of the Euphrates and Tigris rivers has meant that Iraq is subject to frequent floods and droughts.

Once again, irrigated agriculture consumes the greatest proportion of the country's water: 42.7km^3 in 1984 (88.4%), with domestic consumption a mere 1.3km^3 (2.7%). Before the Gulf crisis these figures were forecast to rise to 46.8km^3 (75.3%) and 3.5km^3 (5.6%) in 1995.[16]

Successive governments have undertaken a number of water management schemes on the Euphrates, notably the Haditha dam (1985, 6.4km³ storage capacity) to irrigate 1m ha.[17] The waters of the Tigris are used to irrigate 2.2m ha, mainly using the Mosul dam (10.7km³). The Shatt al-Arab was used to irrigate 105,000ha, but the current picture is uncertain in the light of extensive economic disruption caused by the 1990–1 Gulf War. Before the Gulf War, Iraq was implementing a number of hydraulic projects on the major rivers and their tributaries, notably the Tharthar canal project to divert water from the Tigris into the Tharthar depression and thence, if necessary, into the Euphrates. Iraq felt that these projects would be jeopardized in the event of substantial reductions in flow from Turkey and Syria. Turkey has argued that any temporary shortfalls in Euphrates flows could be compensated to some extent by water from the Tigris.

The long-term aim of Iraq's hydraulic projects was to develop new irrigation networks and bring all suitable land under irrigation by the year 2000. The total cultivable area is 8m ha, of which 4–5m are cultivated in any one year. Salinity affects 65% of all irrigated land in Iraq; between 1937 and 1957 20% of the land under irrigation was abandoned because of salinity and waterlogging caused partly by soil type, partly by over-irrigation. Before the Gulf War Iraq had embarked on some studies to develop sprinkler and drip irrigation systems and build long-term storage dams to offset anticipated reductions in Tigris and Euphrates flows. Iraq fears that GAP and hydraulic projects in Syria will reduce Euphrates flows by two-thirds to 11km³/yr; the figure could be as low as 7km³ which could irrigate only 36.8% of lands watered in 1990. Furthermore, water quality could decline below 1,000ppm because of contamination by chlorides, fertilisers and pesticides from return flows upstream.

It can be argued that Iraq's water-management programme was unrealistic. The Iraqi economy is entirely oil-based, accounting for 99.6% of foreign earnings and any attempts at economic diversification are cosmetic. On the basis of existing systems the best Iraq can hope for is modest food security; with properly managed irrigation systems, in addition to a large area of rain-fed cultivation in the north of the country, Iraq has potential for self-sufficiency in agriculture. The agricultural sector was hit hard in the 1980s by shortages of agricultural labour, the result of urbanization (75% of the population of 18m live in cities) and military service in the Iran–Iraq and Gulf wars.

By the mid-1980s Iraq was importing 80% of its food requirements by value (70% by calories); in 1987 food accounted for 26.7% of imports by value.[18]

Whilst agricultural production was severely disrupted and a great deal of hydraulic infrastructure destroyed as a result of bombing during the Gulf War, the government strategy of self-sufficiency in cereal production averted wider social calamities. This has reinforced the feeling among many economic policy-makers in the region that depending on large volumes of food imports increases economic and political vulnerability, even though, under normal circumstances, importing food is a cheaper option in oil economies, certainly in terms of water. Under normal circumstances, Iraq was well-advised to continue to rely on food imports and could afford to do so economically. On 6 August 1990, after the UN Security Council imposition of economic sanctions against Iraq, the Ministry of Agriculture launched a campaign to increase the cultivated area and cereal production by 50%. Farmers were ordered to plant 80% of their land with cereal crops, and cereal production in 1990 did increase by 70% over the 1987–9 period. Food rationing was introduced in September 1990 and is still in force.

Bombing by coalition forces caused extensive damage to Iraq's infrastructure. Only one main water project, the Darbandikhan dam, emerged relatively unscathed, suffering 50% damage. The Dokan and Haditha dams were 75% destroyed and the Ramadi barrage, Saddam and Samarra dams were put out of action altogether.[19] The destruction of dams and pumping installations, water purification plants and power stations has had serious consequences for energy and food production, and for the provision of clean drinking water. Crop failures were widespread in summer 1991 because of shortages of inputs (fertilisers, pesticides, spare parts for machinery and pumps), power failures, restrictions on aerial crop spraying and harvesting in border regions. The wheat and barley harvests in 1991 were down 50% since the previous year and crop yields in 1992 were still low because of continued shortages of inputs.[20] One of the biggest casualties was the date crop, which was contaminated by the discharge of raw sewage into the Tigris.[21] Iraq's current plan to build a 565-km 'third river' between the Tigris and Euphrates is ostensibly aimed at reducing salinity in the agricultural heartland. However, as the scheme will also drain large areas of the southern marshes it is seen as a political move against the local Shi'a community and the Marsh Arabs. Availability of spare machine parts and funds will determine its progress.

Political and economic relations between the riparian states
Bilateral relations between Turkey and Syria have long been uneasy. Consequently, Turkey has been reluctant to make concessions on water issues, feeling that water is a very useful negotiating tool. The two principal sources of friction between the states are: Syria's backing of opponents of the Turkish regime; and, to a lesser extent, Syrian irredentist claims to the province of Hatay. This province, formerly Alexandretta, part of the French mandate of Syria, was ceded to Turkey in 1939. In October 1989 Syrian airforce planes shot down a plane belonging to the Turkish land registry office flying over Hatay, whilst in December 1989 the Syrian Minister of Information stated at

a press conference in Nicosia that Syria still did not recognize Hatay as part of Turkey.

Turkey has accused Syria of supporting Kurdish (PKK), Armenian (the Armenian Secret Army for the Liberation of Armenia – ASALA) and left-wing (*Dev Sol*) guerrillas, especially since the early 1980s. The PKK in particular launched many incursions into Turkey in 1980–5 from Syrian bases and were not significantly diminished by diplomatic pressure or the signing of extradition agreements.

Negotiations on this issue intensified in 1986–7 with the visit to Ankara in March 1986 of the then Syrian Prime Minister Abd al-Rauf al-Qasm. At this point Syrian concern over possible depletion of Euphrates water as a result of GAP was included in the security agenda. Despite agreements, there was little visible slowdown in PKK activities. A security protocol signed by Turkey and Syria in 1987 following a bilateral economic cooperation agreement, which included provisions on the Euphrates river, had little meaning in practice. The PKK centre of operations was moved from Syria to the Beqaa valley in Lebanon which was under Syrian military control. Syria refused to extradite the leader of the PKK, whom it described as a political refugee.

PKK operations from the Beqaa valley continued throughout the late 1980s and early 1990s, causing increased agitation in Turkey. President Özal frequently warned that Turkey would not tolerate terrorism sponsored by its neighbours, and would go so far as to bomb bases in the Beqaa valley if necessary. In October 1987 Özal stated that Euphrates water would be cut off if Syria did not desist from supporting the PKK. Prime Minister Suleyman Demirel has stated repeatedly that his government desires the expulsion of the PKK and *Dev Sol* from the Mahsun Kokmaz training academy in the Beqaa valley: 'Let me say it clearly. We will act against those who try to destroy Turkey. We will not wait until they cause damage. Turkey has the right to take steps against those bases which disturb it and this right is the result of international law'.[22] This 'right' would be exercised with Israeli assistance if necessary. Nevertheless, Turkey is continuing to opt for diplomatic rather than military solutions: on 17 April 1992 the Turkish Minister of the Interior visited Damascus, and following this, a bilateral security agreement was signed and a *Dev Sol* training camp in the Beqaa valley was reportedly closed.[23] On 3 August 1992 Turkish Foreign Minister Hikmet Çetin held talks in Damascus with his Syrian counterpart, Farouq al-Shar'a, and with President Assad: Turkey agreed to respect its commitments on Euphrates water so long as Syria upheld its obligations under the April security accord. Further talks were held in September 1992 between Turkey and Syria at which both sides reiterated their commitment to border security; Syria stated that it had outlawed PKK activities in territory under its control. The long-term significance of these developments remains to be seen.

Turkish–Syrian official economic ties are limited but it is important to note that transit trade, Turkish livestock exports to Syria, and

Syrian cereal exports to Turkey flourished despite political friction. In March 1992 Turkey and Syria signed an agreement on aerial surveys in the border region.

Turkish and Iraqi policies have often coincided on the issue of Kurdish separatism. This has extended to tacit, and even overt, military cooperation, particularly after General Kenan Evren came to power in Turkey after a coup in 1980. Turkey's reprisals against PKK bases in northern Iraq tended to coincide with Iraqi action against the PUK and KDP. In October 1984 Turkey and Iraq signed a 'Hot Pursuit' agreement whereby both sides could 'pursue subversive groups in the territory of the other' up to five km. Turkish raids into northern Iraq were therefore carried out with Iraqi consent, as the Kurds were backed by Iran, with which Iraq was at war. However, Iraq was aggrieved at being excluded from the Turkish–Syrian economic protocol in 1987, especially from discussions on the division of the Euphrates waters. It became gradually less cooperative on border security, and by 1988 the PKK was in effect operating at will from inside northern Iraq. After the end of the Iran–Iraq War, and following the Iraqi suppression of Kurdish dissent in February 1988 (including the chemical attack on the town of Halabja), over 60,000 Kurds fled into Turkey; the Iraqi army was not permitted to pursue them.[24]

During the Gulf War, US air bases at Incirlik were used by the US to attack targets in Iraq. In the aftermath of the war over 400,000 Kurds fled to south-east Turkey, and PKK attacks on military personnel in south-east Anatolia led to Turkish reprisals on bases in northern Iraq on an almost weekly basis in early 1992. Although some restrictions on the use of the Kurdish language and the propagation of Kurdish culture have been lifted in Turkey, there is no indication of any concessions being made regarding political separatism. Turkey remains committed to the destruction of PKK facilities in northern Iraq and has been enlisting the support of other Kurdish parties, notably the KDP which, according to its leader, does not support terrorism.[25]

Turkish–Iraqi economic ties flourished during the 1980s, although with fears on both sides that economic dependence might become excessive. Turkey was the principal conduit for Iraqi oil exports (1.5m barrels/day by 1987), especially after the final closure of the Iraqi–Syrian pipeline in 1982. Not only did Turkey receive 60% of its oil supplies from Iraq, some at a discount, but also substantial transit fees. Many joint economic ventures were undertaken, such as the interconnection of the electrical grid and the building of an international railway to Zakho in northern Iraq. The volume of direct bilateral trade grew tremendously during the Iran–Iraq War; by the end of the war Iraq owed Turkey $2bn.

The UN embargo against Iraq has had serious economic consequences for Turkey: Turkey was Iraq's bridge to Europe, and it had become dependent on Iraqi oil (now supplied mainly by Saudi Arabia). The Turkish pipelines were immediately shut down after the

Iraqi invasion of Kuwait.[26] Nevertheless, there are indications that Turkey is keen to resume trading relations in the near future; Iraq would almost certainly be a consumer of agricultural goods produced in the GAP region.

Relations between Syria and Iraq have been based on mutual suspicion since the ideological split which occurred in the 1960s. They are both nominally ruled by different branches of the pan-Arabist Ba'ath party. Syria and Iraq have accused each other of harbouring regime opponents. In 1980 there were major crackdowns by Saddam Hussein against opposition figures, especially Shi'is, ethnic Turks (Turcomans) and Kurds. The Syrian response was to provide facilities for opposition groups, notably the Iraqi Democratic National Patriotic Front, the PUK and the KDP; Syria supported Iran in the Iran–Iraq War, although there are indications of limited economic cooperation between Syria and Iraq in the period after the Gulf War.

The Water Factor
Disputes over unilateral exploitation of the Tigris and Euphrates and, to a lesser extent, the Asi river between Turkey and Syria have frequently provoked interstate tension. Efforts have continually been made by the parties concerned to reach working arrangements on allocations, although it is fair to conclude that these discussions have reached an impasse. There are no tripartite treaties between the riparian states of the Tigris–Euphrates basin on the allocation or exploitation of the river waters. The 1923 Treaty of Lausanne included a provision that Turkey must consult Iraq before undertaking any hydraulic works. The 1930 Treaty of Aleppo referred briefly to Syrian water rights on the Tigris, while the 1946 Ankara Treaty of Friendship and Good Neighbourliness, signed by Turkey and Iraq, stated that Iraq was to be consulted before Turkey carried out any development projects on the Tigris or Euphrates.[27] In 1962 Syria and Iraq formed a Joint Technical Committee, but its role was limited as no major hydraulic works were undertaken during this period. In the period 1972–3 attempts were made, unsuccessfully, by Syria and Iraq to negotiate an agreement on Euphrates waters.

The period 1974–75 witnessed considerable friction between the riparian states over the exploitation of the Euphrates, as both Turkey and Syria embarked on major dam-building projects. The construction of the Keban dam in Turkey provoked Syrian anxiety and official protest, not because of actual water depletion (the dam is designed for HEP generation and to regulate Euphrates flows), but because of the symbolic value of Turkey's demonstration of its ability to control river flows. The fact that flow regulation may be hydrologically beneficial was politically irrelevant.

The construction of the Tabqa dam in Syria in 1973–4 provoked an aggressive Iraqi response, but coincided with a general deterioration in bilateral relations. The process of filling the Lake Assad reservoir temporarily deprived Iraq of some of the natural flow of the Euphrates: figures given by Syria and Iraq vary, but Iraq claimed it received less than one third of its average annual Euphrates flow (9.4km^3) in 1975, whilst Syria contended that Iraq received 12.8km^3, equivalent to Iraq's annual consumption at the time. In any event, the Syrian authorities contended that Iraq could use water from the Tigris river to make up for any shortfall. Iraq claimed a 'rightful share' of 16.1km^3 of Euphrates water, based on a 1965 World Bank recommendation. In a note to the Arab League Council in April 1975, Iraq complained that Syria was storing far more Euphrates water than it required in Lake Assad for political reasons, which led to the destruction of 70% of Iraq's winter crop. Saudi Arabia was called in to mediate as political and economic relations deteriorated rapidly: Syria and Iraq closed each others' airline offices and airspace, and sent troops to their common border. Syria made no secret of its support for PUK forces and other Iraqi opposition groups. Following Soviet mediation in June 1975 Syria agreed to release additional water from the Tabqa dam and in August of that year accepted a Saudi proposal for the proportional division of Euphrates waters, although this was not followed up.[28] Iraq accused Syria of withholding Euphrates waters on several occasions during the drought-prone 1980s.

Turkey's unilateral decision to proceed with the GAP scheme was perceived as aggressive and insensitive by its downstream neighbours. Such an action demonstrated the lack of an adequate consultative mechanism, although bilateral and multilateral discussions on the water issue have taken place. In 1982 Turkey and Iraq established a Joint Technical Committee, which Syria joined in 1983. The Committee has met regularly for general project discussions and exchange of hydrological data, but it has been unable to solve the problem of competing claims by the riparian states. Existing bilateral agreements are limited in scope.

In July 1987 Turkey and Syria signed a Protocol of Economic Cooperation covering a wide range of issues: oil and gas exploration, banking, livestock transport and customs formalities. Water was one of the principal issues and followed Abd al-Rauf al-Qasm's request for guaranteed minimum Euphrates flows in return for Syrian cooperation on border security. It is important to note that the Protocol was regarded as a temporary arrangement. The text of Article 6 reads:

> During the filling up period of the Atatürk dam reservoir and until the final allocation of the waters of the Euphrates among the three riparian countries, the Turkish side undertakes to release a yearly average of more than 500 cubic metres per second at the Turkish–Syrian border and in cases where the monthly flow falls below the level of 500m^3/sec, the Turkish side agrees to make up the difference during the following month.[29]

Article 7 stated that Turkey and Syria should work together with Iraq to allocate Tigris and Euphrates waters within the shortest possible time. Under Article 9 both states agreed in principle to construct and jointly operate irrigation and HEP projects.The Iraqi Deputy Premier Taha Yasin Ramadan complained to President Özal in Baghdad in April 1988 that Iraq had not been included in negotiations on water. He was reassured by Özal that the 1987 Protocol was temporary, and that a 'real treaty' (a tripartite agreement) would eventually be concluded between the riparian states.

The most serious confrontation between Turkey and its downstream neighbours occurred in January 1990 when Turkey began to divert the Euphrates in order to fill the Atatürk dam reservoir. It was this confrontation and war of words which prompted fears of a Middle East water war. The scenario was portrayed as alarming: Turkey was turning off the taps.

Turkey's decision to impound Euphrates waters from 13 January to 12 February 1990 was controversial because of the assertive way in which it was implemented, despite the guarantees of compensatory flows downstream. At the November 1989 meeting of the Joint Technical Committee, Syria and Iraq argued that two weeks rather than four were sufficient for reservoir impounding, and called for a trilateral agreement on water quotas. Syria complained that only one out of eight 100-MW turbines was functioning on the Tabqa dam. Iraq claimed that the proposed reduction in Euphrates flows would damage irrigation schemes (1.3m ha) and shut down power plants which produced 40% of the country's electricity.[30] Turkey, however, argued that Syria would receive a minimum flow of 120m³/sec from tributaries below the Atatürk dam, as well as additional flows at a rate of 750m³/sec from 23 November to 13 January (Euphrates discharge into Syria averaged 768m³/sec in this period, so during this and the impounding period the average flow would be 509m³/sec within the terms of the 1987 protocol). Turkey also stressed that the impounding was scheduled for the time when Syrian and Iraqi water requirements were lowest, and claimed that the fears disseminated in the Arab media were groundless. The Syrian government protested officially to Turkey and to the Arab League, which consequently called for a just sharing of Euphrates waters and for a reduction in the impounding period. Syrian engineers claimed that the level of the Euphrates fell by three metres in January 1990 between the Turkish border and Lake Assad, thus damaging the winter crop and interrupting domestic water supplies to Aleppo, and that Turkey had not provided sufficient technical details about its plans. Turkish engineers contended that they had done everything possible to minimize damage.

This interruption to the flow of the Euphrates was the first of several envisaged as part of GAP and prompted Syria and Iraq to join forces in calling for a tripartite agreement. On 16 April 1990 Syria signed an accord with Iraq on the allocation of Euphrates waters: Syria would receive 42% and Iraq 58% of annual flows, regardless of quantity. In March and December 1991 Syria protested about temporary reductions in Euphrates flows and reiterated calls for trilateral negotiations on the matter. Syria and Iraq reiterated their call for a trilateral agreement at the most recent meeting of the Joint Technical Committee in Damascus in September 1992, the first since the Gulf War. The meeting ended in deadlock amidst accusations of Turkish intransigence. Turkey argued yet again that its 1987 quota agreement with Syria was equitable and indeed adequate for downstream requirements and that Syria and Iraq should use their water supplies more efficiently.

National security perceptions and prospects for conflict and cooperation
The key issue for the riparian states is to overcome intransigent positions on what constitutes a mutually acceptable legal framework for the utilization of the shared rivers, accompanied by efforts at water conservation. Without these developments international rivers in the region will always be a source of tension.

The role of the Joint Technical Committee should not be underestimated. Although its meetings are infrequent and appear to have made little substantive progress on the question of water sharing, it is a useful channel for communications. Hydrological data are exchanged regularly by telex. Technical cooperation is politically unspectacular but does mitigate confrontational rhetoric. The Committee clearly cannot fully address the security concerns of the cooperating states since they relate to issues other than water.

The principal obstacle to a political settlement is the issue of sovereignty. Turkey adamantly opposes a multilateral agreement on the allocation of Tigris and Euphrates waters as it can see little political or economic gain in this. Turkey remains mistrustful after the failure of past security agreements, in particular those made with Syria. The official view is that the Tigris and Euphrates are sovereign resources and may be exploited as Turkey sees fit. For example, as Prime Minister Demirel stated: 'Water is an upstream resource and downstream users cannot tell us how to use our resource. By the same token oil is an upstream resource in many Arab countries and we do not tell them how to use it'.[31] On another occasion Demirel asserted in a tone reminiscent of arguments in favour of the nuclear deterrent: 'I do not believe in worrying about threats of war resulting from development projects in Turkey. If there is a threat we will repel it. Turkey has deterrence. It will have more deterrence in the coming period. Turkey will build more such works. The more it builds, the fewer threats it will be faced with'.[32]

According to the Turkish government, the Tigris and Euphrates form a single transboundary watercourse and are not international rivers. Any Euphrates shortfalls can therefore be compensated by the Tigris. Less controversially, Turkey argues that there is sufficient water in the Tigris– Euphrates basin for all countries if it is used properly, but contends that Syria and Iraq have been wasting their water resources for many years. Turkey insists that the 1987 agreement on allocation with Syria is permanent and rejects Syrian and Iraqi claims for higher quotas, nearer 700 m³/sec. Turkey no longer promotes itself as a potential Middle East water reservoir, given the growth in national water demand, and is thus unlikely to accede to requests for higher quotas.

Turkey is in favour of *ad hoc* bilateral joint ventures in water and energy development and is prepared to cooperate on such matters as data management and water-saving studies. Water can be an excellent means of regional cooperation: GAP could trigger economic growth throughout the Tigris–Euphrates region. However, Turkey's willingness to include Israel in its list of potential investment partners, has irritated its downstream neighbours, and as long as the PKK remains operational Turkey will be reluctant to make any concessions on water to Syria. This reluctance is also partly linked to the problem of the Asi river. As the river runs mainly through Syrian territory and into the disputed Hatay/Alexandretta region Syria does not consider it to be an international river. Only 25mcm flow into the Hatay region in the summer, prompting complaints by local farmers to the Turkish authorities. As a result, Turkey is planning to build a dam in the area to store surplus winter flows. Turkey has also attempted to link negotiations on the Euphrates to a deal on the Asi river, but Syria has opposed this on the grounds that it would imply de facto recognition of Turkish sovereignty over Hatay. Syrian officials maintain that the 'sovereign' status of the Asi is non-negotiable unless there is a prior agreement on the Euphrates, which it wants all parties to define as an international river.

There are no immediate prospects for the clarification of the legal position regarding the Tigris–Euphrates basin but it would be wrong to predict escalation, given financial and technical considerations. Rivers will not simply be 'turned off'; for instance, during the Gulf War Iraq was not threatened with the diversion of its water supplies from upstream. Neither Syria nor Iraq is in a position to challenge Turkey militarily and, beyond support for rebel groups, they have little leverage other than diplomatic pressure. Of course, the Atatürk dam and other installations are always vulnerable to sabotage and the Turkish government maintains a strong security presence in the area. The PKK has repeatedly declared its opposition to the project, portraying it as theft of Kurdish waters.

Finally, Turkish foreign policy concerns are shifting away from the Middle East. This is reflected in the fate of the Peace Pipeline project, which was championed by President Özal from 1987 until late 1991. It was proposed that two pipelines would transport water from the Seyhan and Ceyhan rivers (a total of six mcm/day): the western pipe would convey water to Syria, Jordan, the West Bank (and possibly

Israel), and thence to the Red Sea coast of Saudi Arabia; the eastern pipe would take water to the Gulf states. Turkey's surplus water would be sold at a cost far lower than that of desalinated water, and it was intended that the pipeline would become a physical bond strengthening cooperation between the states of the region.

The pipeline and its variation, the 'mini pipeline' (which would supply only Syria, Jordan and the West Bank and/or Israel), have been shelved by the Demirel administration in the face of overwhelming opposition from its proposed customers and an official rethink on Turkey's domestic needs.[33] The pipeline would have been extremely vulnerable to sabotage or political pressure. Turkey no longer claims to have a water surplus; indeed Foreign Minister Hikmet Çetin stated in January 1992 at the Moscow multilateral talks:

> Concerning water, we are aware of its growing importance and its regional implications. We see it as an integral element of overall regional cooperation. We are ready to cooperate in this respect, but I must point out that we will do so in accordance with our own priorities and within the limits of our potential. Turkey is not a country which has abundant water resources. We may soon face problems in meeting our own needs.

Turkey will press ahead with its hydraulic works and fend off diplomatic protests with talk of economic cooperation. So long as the issues of border security and Kurdish nationalism have not been resolved one can expect water to be used as a bargaining card. It must be emphasized that although interruptions in the flow of the disputed rivers will punctuate the next decade, they should not be interpreted as harbingers of imminent conflict. They will not have been carried out without technical consultation.

III THE NILE BASIN

The river Nile and its tributaries are shared by nine states with varying claims on its waters and at differing stages of economic development: Egypt, Sudan, Ethiopia, Uganda, Kenya, Tanzania, Rwanda, Burundi and Zaire. The principal causes for concern in the region are environmental and economic: climatic change has resulted in reduced rainfall, leading to lower than average Nile flows and jeopardizing existing hydraulic projects. Egypt and Sudan are the Nile's largest consumers. Egypt does not contribute any water to the Nile system, but with the largest population in the region, it has by far the highest demand for water. It is also the region's most stable political entity, with the strongest economy and military capability. Egypt's long-term economic survival will depend on cooperative development of Nile waters with its upstream neighbours, but such projects are jeopardized by the civil war in Sudan, and by political instability in Ethiopia. The safeguarding of Nile flows is therefore regarded by Egypt as a strategic priority. It has vested interests in a stable *entente* with Sudan and Ethiopia, viewing with suspicion the consolidation of power by the radical Islamic regime in Sudan, and with disquiet the gradual political disintegration of post-Mengistu Ethiopia.

Although integrated Nile river management, widely advocated by hydrologists, might be desirable from a technical point of view, there are no multilateral agreements which take into account the needs of all the basin states, due to Egypt's insistence for many years that its water needs are paramount. The only agreement on Nile waters currently in force is a bilateral treaty concluded between Egypt and Sudan in 1959.

Hydrological profile
The Nile is formed by two main tributaries: the White Nile and the Blue Nile. The headwaters of the upper White Nile are in the East African highlands in Burundi, draining into Lake Victoria. The White Nile flows out through Owen Falls, Lake Kyoga, Kabalega (Murchison) Falls and Lake Mobutu (Albert) in Uganda into Sudan as the Bahr al-Jabal. At least 50% of the discharge of the White Nile ($27km^3/yr$) is lost in the Sudd swamplands of southern Sudan. The headwaters of the Blue Nile are in the Lake Tana region of north-west Ethiopia. The Blue and White Niles converge at Khartoum. The most northerly tributary of the main Nile is the Atbara river; after the Atbara confluence the Nile flows directly through Egypt and drains into the Mediterranean.

The average annual discharge of the Nile at Aswan, Egypt, is $84km^3$ (based on 1900–1959 average natural flow). Eighty-six percent of the discharge of the Nile originates in Ethiopia (the Blue Nile 59%, the Atbara 13% and the Sobat, a tributary of the White Nile, 14%), and 14% originates in the East African equatorial plateau. However, as already noted, most of the water is used by Sudan and Egypt. Under

The River Nile and its tributaries

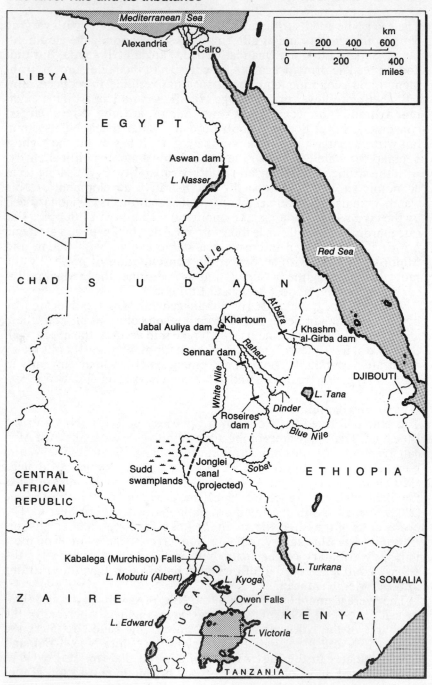

the provisions of the 1959 Egyptian–Sudanese Nile Waters Agreement Egypt was allocated 55.5 km^3, Sudan 18.5km^3 and the remaining ten km^3 were accounted for by mean annual evaporation and seepage losses from Lake Nasser behind the Aswan High Dam.

The region has been undergoing unexpected climatic changes which make predictions of future water availability in the riparian states unreliable. Assumptions about water availability in Egypt especially are having to be modified.[1] Drought in the mid-1980s vividly illustrated the unpredictability of Nile flows and the problems of long-range forecasting. For example, between 1961–4 above-average rainfall over Lake Victoria increased the level of the lake by two metres, thus increasing White Nile flows by 32% above their pre-1961 average until the mid-1980s. Meanwhile, rainfall in Ethiopia steadily declined and this reduced the flow of the Blue Nile by 16%.[2] When White Nile flows returned to their average levels in the late 1980s, having previously compensated for low Blue Nile flows, Egypt and Sudan were hit by water shortages which were alleviated only by unexpectedly heavy rains over Ethiopia and central and eastern Sudan in August 1988.

The Nubian sandstone aquifer is another major regional water resource and falls within the territory of Egypt, Sudan, Libya and Chad. It is a complex aquifer system covering 2.5m km^2 and contains approximately 50,000km^3 of water which is up to 40,000 years old.[3] Libya is the chief exploiter of this resource, followed, on a far smaller scale, by Egypt, Sudan and Chad. The impact on ground-water level and flow of Libya's Great Man-Made River project (see Appendix I) and the consequences for ground-water development in Egypt are not yet fully understood.

National priorities
EGYPT

Before considering the potential for water-related conflict in the Nile basin it is essential to take a careful look at the water and agricultural sector in Egypt. Egypt never ceases to promote itself as the 'gift of the Nile', as it was once described by Herodotus, but its water-management policy is economically controversial.

Rainfall in Egypt is negligible, occurring mainly along the Mediterranean coast in winter (200mm/yr). In addition to its annual quota of 55.5km^3 from the Nile, Egypt uses 6km^3 from Sudan's quota, as Sudan has not yet been in a position to use its full allocation. Egypt would now be reluctant to give up this additional supply. Ground-water reserves are substantial: approximately 300km^3 are available in the Nile Delta and 200km^3 in the Nile valley aquifer, and additional non-renewable fossil reserves are found in the Western Desert (including the New Valley oases and the Oweinat, a remote oasis in the south-west), the Eastern Desert and Sinai peninsula. Only a very small proportion of this is economically recoverable and has to be managed with great care to prevent uncontrollable decline in the water table or saline water intrusion. Current ground-water abstraction in the Nile valley and delta is 2.9km³, well below 4.9km³, the annual rate of recharge. Some reports estimate that 1,042km³ ground-water are recoverable annually at an economic rate in the New Valley.[4] Some drainage water, which would otherwise flow into the Mediterranean, is used for cultivation: estimated current use is 4.7km³, of which 2.4km³/yr is mixed with freshwater and used for irrigation in the southern delta. A total of 13.2km³ would normally drain into the sea and all flow beyond the Edfina barrage (5km³) is non-exploitable, used to maintain navigational levels and for irrigation during the canal maintenance period each January.

Egypt faced an unprecedented water deficit in the summer of 1988, but whether this will lead to a re-evaluation of the country's water policy remains to be seen. It may have forced the recognition of supply limitations but has not curtailed plans for land reclamation. In July 1988 the volume of live storage in Lake Nasser behind the Aswan dam had fallen to 41.1km³; the level of the lake was only three metres above its 'red line' of 147 metres, at which the HEP turbines are shut off or irrigation water supply has to be curtailed drastically. The rains in August 1988 brought live storage up to 75.3km³ amidst great relief. By November 1991 the level was a more reassuring 94.4km³.

In 1990 over 80% of water in Egypt from all sources was used in irrigated agriculture, consuming approximately 38km³/yr (excluding two km³ loss from irrigation canals through evaporation). The majority of water delivery systems are inefficient so that water loss in the irrigation network averages 40–60%. The domestic sector accounted for three km³ with network losses reaching 55% of total deliveries. Industry consumed 4.7km³, while 1.8km³ was used for maintaining the river level for navigation purposes, particularly for tourist cruisers.[5]

Egypt's population is set to increase steadily from 58.3m (mid-1992) to 70m by the year 2000. Population growth during the 1980s averaged 3% per annum and is currently 2.4% per year.[6] Existing water supplies cannot hope to meet expected demand which is forecast to reach 65km³ by the turn of the century (54.4km³ for irrigation, three km³ for domestic supply and eight km³ for industry).[7] Other forecasts suggest that Egyptian agriculture will require an additional 12.7km³ water annually if all land reclamation projects proceed as planned.[8]

Some progress has been made in the use of marginal water resources, notably drainage water and waste water (recycled effluent), and by desalination of brackish and sea-water and small-scale rain-water harvesting. It is hoped that drainage water recycling will increase to ten km³ with storage in Lake Manzala and Lake Barlus near the Mediterranean coast. Waste-water irrigation schemes have been planned for some time; pilot projects were undertaken as early as 1915. The Greater Cairo waste-water project is designed to harness 1.93km³/yr of effluent by 2010. However, use of treated sewage must be carefully monitored to prevent bacterial contamination or clogging of the soil and irrigation systems. Desalination plants have been built at Hurghada on the Red Sea coast, and at Marsa Matruh on the Mediterranean coast. A pilot salt-water irrigation project has been established at Suda in the Sinai peninsula and there are small rain-water harvesting projects in Marsa Matruh and Siwa oasis. Innovative though they might be, such schemes are experimental and do not address the underlying cause of high water consumption, that is the problem of agricultural expansion.

Egypt has a long tradition of cultivation in the Nile valley and delta and has pursued ambitious plans for land reclamation outside these areas. Since the late nineteenth century a number of dams and barrages have been built on the Nile with the aim of regulating the flow throughout the year to provide water during the low flow season from January to July. Egypt's water policy since the 1960s has centred on over-year storage at Aswan. The Aswan High Dam came onstream in 1970. It was designed to protect against floods and droughts, which it did successfully during the 1970s and early 1980s, to generate HEP and also to extend the irrigated area by 20%. Most importantly, the dam ensures a large measure of Egyptian control over the national water supply, although the dam's economic viability is increasingly questionable. The site itself is controversial, given that evaporation rates in the area are amongst the highest in the world.[9] The accumulation of silt behind the dam has deprived farmers of valuable natural fertilisers and increased river bank and coastal erosion. Furthermore, the importance of hydropower in national electricity generation is declining: the dam now accounts for only 22% of total production. Many argue that the Aswan Dam has outlived its usefulness as a national prestige project and that it is an obstacle to cooperative development between the riparian states.

Approximately 7.4m *feddans* (3.1m ha)[10] are cultivated annually in Egypt, accounting for three percent of the total land area. Of this, 2.4m ha are in the Nile Valley and Delta, the so-called 'Old Lands' and the rest form the 'New Lands' reclamation areas. These New Lands are on the western fringes of the Delta, near the Suez Canal, and in northern Sinai. Extension of the cultivated area, coupled with land reform throughout existing lands, was one of the outstanding ambitions of the Nasser years: between 1960–71 912,000 *feddans* (383,000ha) were reclaimed.[11] At least 25% of these lands have since become unproductive as a result of waterlogging and salinization caused by over-irrigation, and only 30% could be considered economically productive. Land reclamation restarted in 1978, and throughout the 1980s was considered to be a priority in five-year investment plans.

The long-term national economic goal is the reclamation of 3m *feddans* (1.26m ha); 919,000 *feddans* (385,000ha) are scheduled for reclamation under the third five-year plan, which began in July 1992. Northern Sinai is to receive 3 km^3/yr of Nile waters via the al-Salam pipeline under the Suez Canal, with the aim of reclaiming 400,000ha of land. Most new projects will rely to a great extent on recycled drainage water. Desert reclamation using ground-water continues in the New Valley oases, despite problems with sinking water tables, but the actual land reclaimed in the entire country has been well below targets.[12] Desert reclamation has not been abandoned, however. The remote Oweinat desert reclamation scheme (currently 2,000 *feddans*) aims to irrigate 85,000 *feddans* (33,700ha), eventually using Nubian sandstone ground-water.[13]

The practical problems of land reclamation are both formidable and costly, and vividly demonstrate economic arguments against horizontal agricultural expansion in arid lands. First, irrigation networks require frequent overhauling and regular maintenance: the most widely-used irrigation method is flood or basin irrigation with drip and sprinkler systems being used only in New Lands. Efficiency is as low as 40% in some areas. Over-irrigation is a widespread phenomenon (in al-Fayyoum oasis, for example, the water allocation per *feddan* was 7,000–8,000m³ in 1990, whereas it is claimed that only 4,500m³ were actually required). Farmers are still reluctant to irrigate at night.[14] In northern Sinai farmers have complained about maldistribution of water by local authorities and about the lack of training in the use of more sophisticated irrigation methods.[15] In 1982 the Ministry of Irrigation (now the Ministry of Public Works and Water Resources) began a programme of canal repairs. Some conservation methods were introduced in 1988 to reduce seepage by lining canals, funding for which was obtained from the World Bank and the International Development Agency.

Second, sandy soils in desert reclamation areas require far more water per unit area than the alluvial soils of the Delta and produce virtually no return flows. Third, land reclamation projects have often been implemented by disaffected officials and untrained personnel: in northern Sinai, for example, land was given to veterans of the 1973 Arab–Israeli war rather than to farmers from the Delta. Finally, approximately 20,000 *feddans* of agricultural land are lost each year to urban encroachment: it is estimated that urban expansion since the building of the Aswan High Dam has claimed almost 900,000 *feddans*, close to that reclaimed for cultivation.

Egyptian agricultural policy has always been highly interventionist, which has adversely affected productivity. Moves are currently under way, as part of the IMF-sponsored economic reconstruction programme, to liberalize the agricultural sector by reducing subsidies on inputs, ending guaranteed (low) producer prices and compulsory cotton cultivation, and by changing the cropping pattern in favour of less water-intensive, higher-value crops. In the mid-1980s *berseem* (clover, used as animal seed) covered 70% of the agricultural area. Other crops such as rice, sugar-cane and cotton, are very water-intensive; rice, for instance, uses 18% of annual water supplies.

Moves are under way, however, to reduce cotton and rice areas substantially and to convert sugar-cane to less water-intensive sugar-beet production.[16] The changing approach to cotton production will affect government taxation policy, particularly indirect taxes on water use.

Water pricing, widely advocated by the World Bank, *inter alia*, as the most effective tool for regulating water consumption by farmers, is an extremely sensitive issue in Egypt. There is no tradition of water pricing in the Egyptian Old Lands, where Nile water is regarded by many farmers as a divine gift. Water has been subsidized at levels of $5–$10bn/yr, largely as a means of indirectly increasing rural incomes to counteract rural–urban migration. Establishing a basis for water pricing will be difficult: if volume-related, then a modern water-metering system must first be devised. If related to crop value then it could easily be seen as a land tax and would not necessarily encourage efficient use. Prices must be within the reach of smallholders (95% of farms are under five *feddans*, or 2.1ha) and there is also the question of whether the cost should cover storage and delivery, and environmental damage. Urban water prices have been increased by 20% to cover the cost of sewage treatment, with higher levies on hotels and other tourist establishments, but implementation has been hampered by the large number of defective meters and the lack of meter-readers. It makes little sense to introduce water pricing without first rehabilitating, and in some cases installing, the basic infrastructure.[17]

Egypt's agricultural expansion programme has been largely motivated by concern over the country's growing food deficit. Since 1974 Egypt has had to import the bulk of its staple food requirements (especially wheat, rice and maize) and this trend continues despite all efforts at boosting domestic production. In 1991 Egypt imported two-thirds of its food requirements at a cost of $4bn; wheat and flour accounted for 6.5m tonnes/yr (domestic production was 4.8m tonnes – 37% self-sufficiency), and consumption was forecast to reach 11m tonnes by the year 2000.[18] Wheat is grown domestically, but over 80% is used in animal feed. Egypt is self-sufficient in fruit and vegetables and is able to export the excess. The Ministry of Agriculture admits that self-sufficiency in cereal production is not practicable, but insists on a minimum level of food security (50% of wheat production 'whatever the cost'). The viability of agricultural expansion is therefore questionable from an economic point of view; although it is clearly perceived as vital to the national interest. Nor can its social implications be overlooked. The agricultural sector employs a substantial proportion of the labour force (35% in 1990).[19] Furthermore, the ultimate aim of land reclamation schemes in remote areas is to disperse a population which inhabits only 4% of the land; pressure on resources and the infrastructure in these areas is becoming intolerable. The question remains, however, whether enough water will be available for all of these schemes. At most, Egypt can hope to recover 10–12km³ water annually through recycling and rehabilitation on a national level.

In the long term, supply can only be increased through the recovery of Nile waters in upstream states. The Jonglei Canal in Sudan, a project begun in 1976 with the aim of bypassing the Sudd swamps, was expected to yield an additional 4.8km³ annually, to be shared equally between Egypt and Sudan. The construction of the canal was halted by the renewed outbreak of civil war in southern Sudan, and it is unlikely to be completed before the end of the 1990s. Other water storage projects have been envisaged for the upper White Nile and the Blue Nile, but they are nowhere near the implementation stage and, in any event, depend on a far larger measure of cooperation between the Nile basin riparians than is evident at present. Should all these projects be implemented and Egypt given priority in water allocation (as has so far been the case with agreements on Nile waters), the most Egypt can expect is an additional 18km³/yr.[20]

SUDAN
Sudan is divided into two main climatic regions: the northern and central areas which are hot and dry and do not have regular annual rainfall, and the south which has marked dry and rainy seasons where rainfall can reach 1,600mm/yr. The average annual discharge of the White Nile at Mogren to the south of Khartoum is 26km³ whilst that of the Blue Nile and its tributaries, the Rahad and Dinder, is 51km³ and that of the Atbara river 12km³. The Blue Nile and Atbara flows are markedly seasonal, almost all occurring from August to December. The Nubian sandstone aquifer also covers northern Sudan but exploitation is limited. The potential yield of wells at Umm Rawaba is 2km³/year. Current ground-water use is estimated at 0.3km³/yr in the Northern Province; it is used for irrigation and domestic supply in conjunction with or as an alternative to Nile water.[21]

Sudan receives 18.5km³ under the 1959 Nile Waters Agreement; however, it only uses approximately 12.5km³ annually. Over 80% is used in irrigation schemes, especially on the Blue Nile Gezira-Managil cotton growing project, in sugar-cane plantations on the White Nile and at Khashm al-Girba on the Atbara, the site of the resettlement area for people displaced after the Aswan High Dam was built and Lake Nasser filled. A number of dams have been built in Sudan: at Jabal Auliya, Sennar, Roseires and Khashm al-Girba, storing approximately eight km³ and generating the bulk of Sudan's electricity. However, their storage capacity is being rapidly diminished through siltation.[22] Sudan has been studying the possibility of a multipurpose dam at Merowe near the Fourth Cataract of the Nile, to become operational after 1998. If water is to be used for irrigation (even though the dam itself will flood existing agricultural land), then Egypt will insist on consultation.

Sudan has been developing irrigated agriculture since the early part of the century: under the Anglo-Egyptian Condominium, Sudan became a major exporter of cotton. In the mid-1970s Sudan came to be seen by its Arab neighbours, particularly Saudi Arabia, as a potential 'bread-basket' to counteract the growing Middle East food deficit. However, misguided cropping patterns and infrastructural weakness put an end to several grandiose cultivation schemes.

Sudan's agricultural sector does have great potential if suitably managed, but it needs a great deal of investment in the most basic infrastructure. The country's cultivated area is approximately 11.2m ha, of which 9.5m ha are rain-fed. Most agricultural activity is along the principal rivers, on the central clay plains and in the savanna. Potential arable land is estimated at 35m ha, with an additional 100m ha suitable for grazing land. Livestock production in Sudan has expanded recently with growing demand from Saudi Arabia and the Gulf states, but its greatest constraint is drought and the lack of extension services. The agricultural sector employs 61% of the workforce (1989);[23] two-thirds of the population is still engaged in subsistence farming, mostly in the southern savanna belt which has an annual rainfall of 440–800mm. Agriculture accounts for 36% of GDP and 95% of exports. Cotton has been Sudan's principal export crop over the past 50 years, although the area under cotton is being reduced by the present government in favour of food crops.

The combination of prolonged drought and population displacement (four million people) caused by civil war has brought about widespread food shortages in many regions of Sudan. Domestic production of cereal crops declined in the 1980s, from 5.5m tonnes in 1988 to 2m tonnes in 1989 and 1990, and 3.8m (est.) in 1991. The biggest problem, however, was not availability but maldistribution, especially in the southern provinces. Cereal imports have increased steadily despite famine predictions, whilst the government continues to announce food surpluses and encourage urban dwellers to return to the land. A number of irrigation extension schemes are under consideration, together with increases in reservoir capacity. Domestic water consumption is negligible (few villages have running water), but is forecast at two km^3/yr if urbanization continues at its present rate.

Sudan's economic and political situation remains precarious which will place in jeopardy any planned irrigation developments and proposed hydraulic works, affecting the upper White Nile in particular. By the end of 1989 Sudan's external debt was $13bn and the country was on the verge of being declared a Non-Cooperating state by the IMF because of loan defaulting. Part of the problem is the country's dependence on imported oil, compounded by its political isolation in the region. The government of Omar Hassan al-Bashir, which came to power in a military coup in June 1989 and is vigorously backed by the radical National Islamic Front, has been receiving support from Libya, Iraq and Iran. Furthermore, it is pursuing an increasingly aggressive and successful campaign against the rebellion by the Sudanese People's Liberation Army (SPLA) in the south. The intermittent civil war, the latest phase of which began in 1983, has not only thwarted hydraulic and other development projects in the south, but has also consumed a substantial portion of the government budget. The southern insurgents, fighting against what they regard as decades of neglect (especially in the provision of basic infrastructure), oppose the imposition of Islamic Law to a region which is non-Muslim, and demand authority over the exploitation of indigenous resources which they claim have been used solely for the benefit of the north.

The Upper Nile water recovery projects may be summarized as follows: Jonglei I involved the building of a 360-km canal from Bor to Malakal on the White Nile to divert 20–25mcm/yr to recover 4.8km^3 (measured at Aswan), which would otherwise be lost through evaporation in the Sudd (total evaporation loss 14km^3). Jonglei II required the building of a parallel bypass canal and a reservoir at Murchison Falls in Uganda on Lake Mobutu (Albert); this would yield a further 4.25km^3 at Aswan. Building canals through the Bahr al-Ghazal basin (evaporation loss 12km^3) could yield approximately five km^3, whilst draining the Machar marshes and Sobat basin (evaporation loss 19km^3) to the east of the White Nile near the Ethiopian border could recover an additional 4.4km^3 with potential storage at Gambela on the Baro tributary of the Sobat in Ethiopia. Hydrological data for most of these areas are speculative.[24]

Environmental and political concerns, as well as technical difficulties, have so far hindered the implementation of these projects. Jonglei I was particularly controversial: the Nilotic population of the Sudd region felt that they had not been properly consulted about the impact that the canal would have on their environment or livelihood, which depended on pastoralism. The canal project envisaged substantial reductions in the swamp on which livestock depended, and would form a barrier to livestock and indeed wildlife migration. Furthermore, there was concern that affected villages would not be satisfactorily connected to road networks, and promises to supply pipes for drinking water and irrigation had not been honoured. It was widely believed that the scheme was more beneficial to the people of northern Sudan and Egypt. Work on the canal, 267km of which had already been built, was stopped by the SPLA in February 1984, although the French construction company, CCI, has expressed its willingness to resume work if the political situation improves. Funding from international aid agencies is unlikely to be available, however, given shifts in opinion about the exploitation of wetlands.

Building a storage dam at Kabalega (Murchison) Falls would flood large areas of the National Park, Uganda's prime tourist attraction, and would lead to the loss of large swamplands in the Sudd with no appreciable benefits to the local inhabitants. The impact on the local economy of the projects in the Bahr al-Ghazal basin and the Machar marshes would have to be carefully assessed.

THE EAST AFRICAN RIPARIANS

The East African Nile riparians have not, to date, exploited their share of the river system to a significant extent. None of the states concerned has a comprehensive master plan for the use of their water supply, most of which does not come from the Nile system. In Uganda, the demand for water for irrigation is negligible and total present water needs are estimated at 2.2km^3, possibly increasing to three km^3 by the year 2000.[25] A 1987 FAO survey concluded that Uganda's irrigation potential was 400,000ha; this would require approximately six km^3/yr of water but could not realistically be envisaged until the middle of the next century. Uganda has more promising HEP potential, especially on the Upper White Nile between Lakes Kyoga and Mobutu, which could be exported in return for hard currency.

Proposals have been put forward in Kenya and Tanzania for the utilization of water from Lake Victoria for irrigation (the Vembere Steppe in central Tanzania, also using water from the Kagera river, and the Kerio valley in Kenya); Kenya and Tanzania could use one km^3/yr. Burundi and Rwanda do not envisage the exploitation of Nile waters; Zaire is considering using the Nile to create HEP for export to Egypt.[26] None of these projects can be expected to materialize in the short to medium term.

ETHIOPIA

Ethiopia's water supply compares favourably with that of its neighbours. Total surface water supply is 111.6km^3, of which 54.4km^3 are exploitable. There are 14 river basins; 11 of these transport approximately 100km^3/yr across Ethiopia's borders. Estimated ground-water potential is 2.6km^3/yr. Yet Ethiopia's relatively abundant resources are poorly distributed: one-third of Ethiopia (just over 40m ha) is drought-prone, whilst 540,000ha are liable to flood. Only 17% of the country's population receives potable running water and total piped water consumption is estimated at 74mcm/yr.[27]

The annual discharge of the Blue Nile, which rises in Lake Tana in the north-western highlands, is approximately 51km^3 (most of this contributed by tributaries below the lake), but it is not yet exploited to any significant extent. The limited irrigation projects undertaken so far are in areas to the east of Addis Ababa, such as the Awash valley in the Shewa and Hararghe regions. Ethiopia's traditional geopolitical orientation has always been towards the Horn of Africa and the Red Sea rather than the Nile basin. Agricultural development of the west is becoming more likely, however, as a result of population growth, although governments have not been in a position to fund irrigation projects. It has been estimated that out of a total land area of 130m ha (1.3km^2), including Eritrea, 63m ha are suitable for cultivation, with 7m currently under cultivation and 3.7m ha potentially irrigable.[28] Agriculture employs 80% of the labour force and accounts for 40% of GDP and 90% of export earnings.[29] Ethiopia lacks a comprehensive water and agricultural management programme: there are no water pricing or cost recovery policies and the performance of irrigation projects is poor because of unlined canals, no night or weekend irrigation and a shortage of trained personnel. Of the cultivated area, 94.7% is owned by small farmers, but under the Mengistu regime the majority of credits were given to state-run cooperatives.[30]

Ethiopia has considerable HEP potential which is so far vastly underutilized: existing installed capacity is 400MW whilst potential capacity is 8,380MW, 53% of the HEP potential of the Nile basin. Most of this potential lies in the Blue Nile basin: the river drops 1,786 metres in the 900km from Lake Tana to the Sudanese border, although the steep slopes present a major obstacle to dam-building. Moreover, the best sites for HEP dams are a long way from the main centres of consumption.[31]

Ethiopian water projects will only become a cause for concern to Sudan and Egypt if significant amounts of water are abstracted from the Blue Nile without prior consultation. Conversely, an integrated water-management project involving storage in the Ethiopian highlands has long been viewed as the most effective means of controlling Nile flows for various uses and would be preferable to existing reservoirs, particularly the Aswan Dam with its excessive evaporation rates (a depth of 1m/year in the Ethiopian highlands compared with 3m/year at Aswan). Proposals for over-year storage of Blue Nile flows at Lake Tana were submitted in 1904, 1927 and 1959.

The most comprehensive study was undertaken by the US Bureau of Reclamation (USBR) in 1958–63. The USBR study covered not just the main channel but the whole of the Blue Nile basin; most of the HEP projects were on the main channel and the irrigation projects were in the plateau valleys on tributaries around Lake Tana, along the Sudanese–Ethiopian border and on the Anchar and Finchaa tributaries. A total of 33 projects were detailed, which would lead to the irrigation of 434,000ha and the installation of 6,965MW of HEP capacity. Total water requirement from the Blue Nile and its tributaries, the Rahad and Dinder, was estimated at 6.367km^3.

Only two of these projects have been realized to date: on the Finchaa in 1972 and at the Tis Issat barrage on the Blue Nile, both for power generation only. Ethiopia has at various times revived the idea of Blue Nile irrigation projects, notably at the UN international conference on water at Mar del Plata in Argentina in 1977, and at the 1981 UN conference on Less Developed Countries. Egypt has always interpreted such declarations as a sign of hostile intent. In the short to medium term, Ethiopia could realistically be expected to use no more than two to four cubic kilometres of Blue Nile flows if it goes ahead with a concerted management programme, but this is unlikely in the short term.[32] It is doubtful that the full range of projects will go ahead in the near future since costs are estimated to be at least $50 bn over 30–40 years and would need to be covered by external aid.[33]

Water negotiations

The Nile river basin is neither a cohesive geopolitical entity nor a community of economic interests. Beyond the river system there is little to bind the riparian states. This, together with Egyptian security perceptions, has proved an insurmountable obstacle to cooperative development of water resources and multilateral discussions.

Inter-riparian cooperation has so far been limited to Egypt and Sudan and all international agreements relating to the Nile have given priority to Egypt's 'historic rights'. The Aswan High Dam is above all a guarantee of Egypt's hydrological security and this consideration so far overrides any criticisms about its effectiveness as a water-regulating mechanism. However, no long-term political or technical solution to Egypt's water demands, or basin-wide water-management scheme is possible without the involvement of Ethiopia.

Britain, as the colonial power in Egypt and Sudan, sought primarily to protect Egypt's claims to priority use of Nile waters. The 1891 Anglo-Italian agreement on spheres of influence in East Africa stated that no irrigation works were to be undertaken on the Atbara river 'which might sensibly modify its flow into the Nile'. In the Anglo-Ethiopian treaty of 1902 Ethiopia pledged not to construct any works on the Blue Nile, Lake Tana or Sobat river to arrest Nile flows except with the agreement of Britain or Sudan. In the 1950s Ethiopia argued that this treaty was never ratified and therefore was non-binding. In an Exchange of Notes with Britain in 1925 the Italian government undertook not to build any hydraulic works on the headwaters of the Blue or White Nile, accepting the acquired hydraulic rights of Egypt and the Anglo-Egyptian Sudan. In an agreement in 1906 the administration of the Belgian Congo affirmed that no works would be constructed on rivers draining into Lake Albert without Sudanese consent.

The Nile Waters Agreement of May 1929 between Egypt and Britain (representing Sudan, Kenya, Tanzania – then Tanganyika – and Uganda) was based on the assumption that Egypt's utilization rights were paramount. Egypt was allocated 48km^3 and Sudan 4km^3 annually (32km^3 were not allocated). Egypt also received all 'timely water' during the January–July low flow period and was permitted to monitor upstream dam-building projects and to veto them if they contravened the national interest. The East African states were to forgo all claims to Nile waters, but the treaty was never invoked or applied in Kenya or Tanzania, and both states argued that it had lapsed on independence.

Egypt was actively involved in the Owen Falls dam agreement of 1949 in cooperation with Uganda and agreed to compensate Kenya and Tanzania for any adverse consequences. The most comprehensive treaty to date is the 1959 Agreement for Full Utilisation of the Nile Waters between Egypt and Sudan. Flows were allocated on the basis of 84km^3 at Aswan as detailed above. Egypt would go ahead with the building of the Aswan dam and compensate displaced local inhabitants, and Sudan would build a dam at Roseires. Any additional water recovered by joint projects on the Upper White Nile was to be shared equally between the two sides. A bilateral Permanent Joint Technical Commission was established; the two sides were also committed to a united front in negotiations on Nile waters with third parties. Britain, the Belgian Congo, the East African states and Ethiopia were not consulted over the final terms of the Nile Waters Agreement and their water rights not mentioned explicitly.

Although the question of riparian rights has still not been resolved satisfactorily there is a degree of consultation between the states concerned. The UN-sponsored Hydromet survey project of 1961, which evaluated the water balance of the Lake Victoria catchment area, was backed by Egypt, Sudan, Tanzania, Kenya and Uganda and later extended to include Rwanda and Burundi. A USAID-sponsored Hydromet survey was begun in 1990. A number of water agreements have been signed between the East African states. A multilateral technical commission was established by all states except Ethiopia in 1967. In 1978 Tanzania, Rwanda and Burundi formed the Kagera Basin Development Organisation, and were joined by Uganda in 1981.

The *Undugu* (meaning 'fraternity' in Swahili) group, which included all states except Ethiopia, was formed in 1983 under the auspices of the Organisation for African Unity (OAU) and has held regular meetings to discuss frameworks for cooperation on the exchange of data and interconnecting electricity grids. It was vigorously backed by UN Secretary General Dr Boutros-Boutros Ghali. Yet *Undugu's* effective powers are limited: it is hardly a grouping of states with equal bargaining powers and its agenda is still largely dictated by Egypt.

Political and economic relations between Egypt, Sudan and Ethiopia
Egypt's relations with Sudan have always been influenced by concern over Nile flows; as a result Egypt has maintained an active interest in political developments in Sudan. The radical Islamic character of the Bashir government in Sudan has prompted fears of Sudanese support for Islamic opposition groups in Egypt; the Egyptian government has repeatedly accused Sudan of harbouring and training Islamic radical groups. During the Gulf War bilateral relations were strained as Egypt backed the anti-Iraq coalition whilst Sudan openly supported Saddam Hussein. Egypt has given military assistance to the SPLA and provided sanctuary for opponents of the Bashir government, notably the former Commander-in-Chief of the armed forces, General Fathi Ahmad Ali, and a collection of opposition figures known as the National Democratic Alliance. Over one million Sudanese live in Egypt.

Tension has flared up recently over the disputed region of Halaib on the Red Sea coast: according to the terms of a 1899 treaty, the area lies in Egyptian territory, but under a 1902 accord it is administered by Sudan. Upon independence in 1956 Sudan's claims to sovereignty over the area were followed by unsuccessful attemps at annexation. In December 1991 the Sudanese government granted an exploration concession to the International Petroleum Company of Canada, a move which Egypt denounced as illegal, especially in the light of Egypt's own plans for offshore oil exploration in the Halaib area. Egypt has announced plans to resettle 4,500 families from the Nile valley in the area and maintains that the issue can be settled amicably. The legal position is not clear, but Halaib's recent prominence can be seen as an expression of continued disquiet.[34] Egypt has also expressed concern over the growing links between Sudan and Iran.

Sudan is in desperate need of cheap oil supplies and its government has been anxious to improve ties with Libya and Iran. Several food-for-oil agreements have been signed with Libya. In October 1991 Sudan signed a technical cooperation agreement with Iraq, and two months later signed a comprehensive trade agreement with Iran under which Iran would supply 100,000 tonnes of oil per month and cover Sudan's military costs until the defeat of the southern rebels.

Throughout the war of words which has intensified between the two countries, Egypt and Sudan have been careful to emphasize the notion of the unity of the Nile valley. No Sudanese government has ever threatened Egypt with a 'water weapon' and bilateral technical discussions on water issues take place regularly. The issue of Nile co-ownership is always raised in times of political tension as a reminder of the need to preserve a degree of political cooperation.

Despite political tensions, Egypt and Sudan have a long-standing record of economic cooperation, particularly in the agricultural sector. The Egyptian Ministry of Agriculture still offers training courses for Sudanese agronomists. Egypt has invested in joint ventures in cereal cultivation and animal husbandry and has supplied seed strains. Egyptian–Sudanese bilateral trade is minimal, however: only 2.6% of Sudan's exports are from Egypt and it exports a mere 3.3% of its annual production to Egypt.

Relations between Egypt and Ethiopia were generally strained during the Mengistu regime, but are warming to a limited extent under the government of Meles Zenawi, leader of the Eritrean People's Revolutionary Democratic Front (EPRDF). There is little to link the states other than Egypt's concern over the use of Blue Nile waters. Egypt and Ethiopia have traditionally been backed by different powers and the Nile question used as political leverage.

During the 1950s, when Nasser was in power in Egypt, Haile Selassie's administration in Ethiopia received aid from the US; the US Bureau of Reclamation study was perceived as a warning to Nasser to moderate his pan-Arabist ambitions and threats against Israel. In the mid-1970s, after President Sadat had expelled his Soviet advisers and turned to the US for economic and military assistance, Mengistu replayed the water card. Soviet advisers conducted feasibility studies in the Lake Tana area whilst the government proclaimed that Ethiopia had the right to exploit its natural resources. At the UN Conference on Water at Mar del Plata in 1977 Ethiopia announced that it was about to irrigate four km³ of the Blue Nile valley,[35] a decision partially influenced by irritation at Egyptian support for Somalia during the Ogaden War. In response, Sadat threatened to bomb any diversion projects if they were built. In 1979 Mengistu denounced Sadat's plans to export Nile waters to Egypt via a Sinai canal and threatened to reduce Blue Nile flows in retaliation.

Egypt has accused Ethiopia at various times of cooperating with Libya and Israel to build dams on the Blue Nile which would be detrimental to Egypt's national interest. However, although Israeli engineers have advised on irrigation projects in the east of the country there is no evidence that any schemes on the Blue Nile have gone ahead with Israeli assistance. Neither Israel nor Ethiopia has any long-term interest in antagonizing Egypt in this way and it is questionable whether Israel alone would have the requisite funds for such projects or that the US would support them.[36] Indeed, a gradual diplomatic *rapprochement* is under way, as Egypt forges diplomatic and economic links with Ethiopia and Eritrea.

Following the Mengistu era, during which Sudan backed the Eritrean People's Liberation Front, and Ethiopia provided bases for the Sudanese People's Liberation Army, Ethiopia and Sudan have strengthened ties. However, there is little ideological common ground between the two regimes, although both face problems of trying to create a sense of national unity. In December 1991 the Ethiopian–Sudanese border was reopened and plans were announced to improve road links. Sudanese military success against SPLA-held areas in the south is partly attributed to Ethiopian collaboration.

On 23 December 1991 the two sides signed an agreement on peace and friendship which paved the way for economic cooperation, particularly over the use of Nile waters. In Article 4.1.5 Ethiopia agreed to participate 'at a full membership level' in basin-wide initiatives as the principal water contributor, whilst Article 4.1.7 affirmed: 'the two sides will endeavour towards the objective of achieving the formulation of the Nile Basin Organisation taking the interests of all riparian countries with their universal consent'. The practical implications of this agreement are not yet clear since neither Egypt nor Sudan is in a financial position to undertake any major hydraulic works, but it can be interpreted as an assurance by Ethiopia that it respects the riparian rights of its downstream neighbours.

Prospects for conflict and cooperation
Despite a consensus on the need for equitable and economic water utilization, the prospects for cooperation remain limited. Broadly speaking, there are few economic ties between Egypt, Sudan and Ethiopia, and even fewer between them and the other riparians, especially Zaire. Agriculture is Nile-dependent in Egypt and Sudan, but to a far lesser extent in Ethiopia and Uganda. Kenya, Tanzania and the other East African riparians are more interested in the river

basin for fishing, navigation and power generation, and geopolitically they lean towards Central Africa and the Indian Ocean. The Nile basin may be considered an ecological unit by many, but the only common ground between the states concerned is a greater or lesser dependence on international aid. No hydraulic works can be financed without external funding which takes into account consequences for co-riparians.

Nevertheless, a number of problems are far from resolution and whether water-related issues become prominent depends on other political factors as described above. The Egyptian government is inflexibly opposed to changing the provisions of the 1959 agreement so as to safeguard its 'historic entitlement'. Egypt is, however, prepared to invest in joint river management schemes if funds are available.

The long-term possibility of over-year storage in Ethiopia is potentially beneficial to Egypt and Sudan. If the USBR projects were to be fully implemented, then Ethiopia would assume *de facto* control over Blue Nile flows but, given lower evaporation losses, Egypt and Sudan would receive higher water allocations than as a result of the Aswan dam. Flows on the Rahad and Dinder would be reduced by one km^3, if projects were undertaken in Ethiopia. This would adversely affect Sudan's Rahad development scheme and also reduce ground-water recharge in the area. The volume of return flows, however, is difficult to estimate. Overall, Egyptian and Sudanese water quotas would still be higher as the Aswan Dam could be operated at lower levels, thus reducing evaporation.[37] The biggest obstacle and the greatest cause for concern in Egypt is that it would lose control over its water supply and become dependent on the goodwill of an upstream neighbour with whom political relations have often been strained and economic ties virtually non-existent.

The history of water negotiations in the Nile basin is encouraging in so far as such negotiations have been fairly regular. Unilateral appropriation of Nile waters is an unlikely scenario. The greatest threat to regional stability is that Egypt, Sudan and Ethiopia face the prospect of recurring and perhaps worsening drought, which can only be offset by greater efforts at conservation and changes in agricultural planning.

61

IV. LEGAL AND FINANCIAL DIMENSIONS

In order to determine the implications of the Middle East water crisis for national, regional and international security it is worth examining the position of international legal and financial organizations. International law on the use of shared water resources is still open to a variety of interpretations. International organizations such as the World Bank, UN agencies and the EC commission have an active interest in water projects in the Middle East and their perception of the issues and solutions differs to some extent from those of the states concerned.

One of the most difficult issues is the establishment of a precise legal definition of international water resources and agreement on the degree of sovereignty which states have over them. Provisions on the consumptive, that is non-navigational, use of international waters have been developed relatively recently; most bilateral or multilateral treaties drawn up in the nineteenth and early twentieth centuries only dealt with freedom of navigation. There is no consensus on terminology, i.e., whether watercourses flowing across territorial boundaries should be referred to as 'international' or 'transboundary' rivers, or 'international river basins' or 'international river systems', much less on the appropriate definition of shared aquifers. So far, disputes over international waters have been resolved by bilateral or multilateral treaty, if at all.

The question of sovereignty over shared water resources is open to a number of interpretations: the 1895 Harmon Doctrine, invoked during US–Mexican negotiations on the Rio Grande, supported the principle of absolute state sovereignty over its territory and thereby over portions of international rivers in its territory. When the US–Mexican treaty was concluded in 1906, the doctrine was repudiated by the US government yet the principle of absolute territorial sovereignty has on occasion been invoked by upstream states.

The main alternative principle, absolute integrity of a river basin, tends to be favoured by downstream states; according to this, each state renounces exclusive rights to water exploitation. Various international legal associations have attempted to draft guidelines on the use of shared watercourses and their conclusions are broadly based on the concepts of 'equitable utilization' and 'sic utere tuo ut alienam non laedas', i.e., that no state should use or permit the use of its territory to cause appreciable harm to its neighbours. This has been emphasized by the International Law Institute, the International Law Association and Inter-American Bar Association and the International Law Commission of the UN.

For example, at the 1958 New York conference of the International Law Association it was agreed that river systems should be treated as an integrated whole. At its fifty-second conference in Helsinki in 1966 the International Law Association drew up what became known as the 'Helsinki Rules', guidelines for areas where there are no bilateral or multilateral agreements. Article IV states that: 'Each basin State is entitled, within its territory, to a reasonable and equitable share in the beneficial use of the water of an international drainage basin' and this reasonableness is determined by such factors as: topography, general availability of water in a state and climatic conditions, economic and social needs, the population dependent on disputed waters and prior usage (detailed in Article V). The Helsinki rules are not, however, binding on any state.

The UN General Assembly agreed in 1972 on the sovereign right of states to exploit their own resources provided that this did not damage areas beyond the limit of national jurisdiction (the Stockholm Declaration) whilst the 1977 UN Conference on water at Mar del Plata, urged cooperation between river basin states on the basis of 'equality, sovereignty and territorial integrity of all states'.

Since 1959 the International Law Commission has been drafting principles on the non-navigational use of rivers. The latest draft (1991) refers to 'international watercourses' and 'watercourse states'. These states must use water in an 'equitable and reasonable manner' with a view to attaining 'optimal utilisation thereof', and cooperate on the basis of mutual benefit and ecological protection. The combined impact of all these deliberations has not been the emergence of any cogent body of international regulations and such regulations could only come into force if ratified by states.

The few agreements on international river utilization in the Middle East that exist are bilateral and official legal interpretations differ widely. The official position in Turkey is that, as the upstream state on the Tigris and Euphrates 'transboundary' rivers, it does not recognize co-ownership of rivers originating in its territory but claims to be utilizing them in an equitable and reasonable manner. Syria and Iraq emphasize the absolute integrity of the Tigris–Euphrates basin, although Syria does not consider the Asi (shared by Lebanon, Syria and Turkey) to be international. The legal status of the Jordan river and its tributaries has been superseded by *de facto* usage. Israeli exploitation of ground-water originating in the West Bank is widely considered as a violation of its position as an occupying power under the Hague regulations of 1907, the Fourth Geneva Convention (August 1949) and various UN General Assembly Resolutions on sovereignty over the 'human, natural and all other resources and wealth of the occupied Arab territories'.

Even if international principles such as the Helsinki Rules or the International Law Commission proposals are accepted, the next problem is enforcement. Arbitration, through the International Court of Justice or the independent Amsterdam-based International Water Tribunal, is one option and carries strong moral authority, but a far more effective mechanism, particularly in the case of Middle Eastern rivers, is financial pressure.

Funding for hydraulic works from such organizations as the World Bank and the International Development Agency is conditional upon agreement between all riparian states being reached, with the resolution of disputes deemed the responsibility of the state or states requesting the loan. Consequently no World Bank loans were forthcoming for Turkey's GAP or the Syrian–Jordanian Unity (Al-Wahda) dam project. Consideration is also given to the potential economic returns on proposed projects and, increasingly but belatedly, to social and environmental consequences, particularly of large dam building.

There has been a shift of international opinion away from large-scale dam and irrigation projects and the exploitation of wetlands, due to hidden costs such as population displacement, loss of fisheries and potential damage to wildlife. Governments in the region are also coming under pressure to reduce, if not eliminate, subsidies on irrigation. Potential donors have become increasingly concerned about the efficient use of water and the performance of institutions. These factors influence policy recommendations.

Agencies such as the United Nations Development Programme, the UN Environment Programme and the European Commission are recommending that priority should be given to measures which will increase the efficiency of water use. The European Commission in particular favours investment in small-scale, low-technology projects. The key words are sustainability, institutional coordination and cost recovery. As in other areas of international relations donor states and organizations are bound to condition their assistance on congenial behaviour, although in the field of water management, as this Paper has shown, the identification of equitable use and fair practice is difficult. Donor states have a role to play in funding confidence-building measures which riparian states may adopt, such as cooperative ventures in water recovery, irrigation efficiency and joint ventures in hydropower generation. This, in turn, can eventually encourage private sector investment if political risks are thought to have decreased as a result. Outside actors must, however, bear in mind the political effects of the national water strategies which they fund or otherwise endorse both within the states concerned and throughout the region.

CONCLUSIONS: THE AGENDA FOR THE 1990s

In the Middle East a number of water-related economic and strategic issues remain unresolved. These do not necessarily add up to a major threat to regional security but do present a challenge to policy-makers and are a source of tension for two principal reasons.

The first is the sense of national vulnerability. Optimum national water security is unattainable and in any case incompatible with policies of food security or principles of international law. None of the riparian or indeed non-riparian states under consideration in this Paper has achieved direct, exclusive and undisputed control over sources of supply and hydraulic installations. None of the states has yet been able politically to pursue a comprehensive programme of reducing national water consumption, particularly in the agricultural sector.

According to these criteria Jordan and the Gaza Strip face extremely serious water shortages and have very limited control over their sources of supply. Syria and Iraq are anxious about future shortages but have partial or total control over a greater variety of water sources. Israel (in effect incorporating the West Bank and the Golan Heights) and Egypt face serious water deficits but have acquired a degree of control over their supply sources which they are anxious to preserve and reinforce, a policy which may not be sustainable in the long term. Turkey does not face immediate water shortages and has a high degree of control over its national water resources amidst some legal controversy. Only Turkey and Sudan can realistically expect to be self-sufficient in food production, whilst all other states in the region will have to continue to rely on food imports. In the non-riparian oil producing states of the Middle East with low populations, especially Libya and Saudi Arabia, the question is how long oil revenues can continue to bolster agricultural schemes which are little more than prestige projects and which use irreplaceable ground-water resources. Food security is the principal motivation behind desert reclamation schemes in these areas, but in environmental terms such a policy is not sustainable.

The second is the problem of competing demands for transnational water resources and the political context in which they occur. This has been demonstrated in the analysis (detailed above) of water issues in the main river basins of the Middle East.

In the Jordan basin region there are justified concerns about overall availability of water on the basis of present consumption patterns and expected population increase. Water supplies *per capita* in Israel and the Occupied Territories are dwindling rapidly, while in Jordan and Gaza the supply situation is perilous. This has been compounded by inadequate water storage facilities, hence the inability to protect against droughts or flooding, and by abstraction of ground-water at rates exceeding the annual rate of recharge. Water planning in Israel and Jordan is now focusing to varying degrees on low- and high-technology water-recovery methods and improved maintenance of water-delivery systems, accompanied by embryonic public awareness campaigns. Attempts are being made to improve irrigation efficiency. This can only be achieved at a slow pace in the Arab water sector of the Occupied Territories because extensive restrictions on development planning and transfer of funds remain in force. Deteriorating water quality through salinization of ground-water aquifers is widespread, particularly in Gaza. In Lebanon the problem is not so much water supply as distribution. The Litani river has not yet been fully exploited in the south and development is conditional upon general economic conditions and, by extension, on future political arrangements with Syria and Israel.

In Israel and the Jordan basin there is the problem of competing institutions and bureaucracies, already noted. The issue of water allocation to the agricultural sector is controversial, given its lowly position in national economies and the fact that, particularly in the case of Jordan, only very limited food security is attainable. Water pricing as a means of controlling consumption has been introduced more successfully in Israel than in Jordan or Syria where tariffs in no way reflect the real cost of water, although price increases in Israel attract vociferous protests from the agricultural lobby. Moreover, the policy of subsidizing water for Israeli settlers in the Occupied Territories contrasts with the high water charges imposed on the Palestinian population. To many Palestinians, therefore, water pricing is another form of political discrimination.

However, while such pragmatic considerations are essential for tackling the underlying causes of water shortage in the Jordan river system, yet they do not address the problems of authority or perceived water rights. Technical solutions to some extent perpetuate the political impasse. The water agenda is dictated almost entirely by Israel's interests and ambitions, as Israel has assumed de facto sovereignty over the region's river system and much of its ground-water. Israel has made clear that it intends to retain control over the headwaters of the Jordan river and the amount of water which it currently withdraws from the Yarmouk, as well as over the principal aquifers on the West Bank. In return, Israel has offered technological expertise and joint ventures in water recovery, especially desalination. Neither Jordan nor the Palestinian population in the Occupied Territories can expect any concessions on what they perceive to be their water rights in the short to medium term, and Israel has rejected the concept of water sharing by quota (the objective of multilateral discussions in the 1950s). Palestinians maintain that Israeli water policy regarding well-drilling and use of water for irrigation on the West Bank, as well as access to hydrological data, violate international laws governing military occupation. Israel, however, contends that relaxation of such restrictions would lead to mismanagement and strategic vulnerability.

Jordanian economic development in the Jordan valley is an encouraging sign of political stability, yet Jordan's almost total dependency on water supplies from beyond its borders is a very great cause for concern. The country's downstream position on the Jordan river and, particularly, the Yarmouk river has left it in a poor negotiating position with regard to Israel but, more importantly, to Syria whose development projects on the upper Yarmouk river have greatly reduced the viability of the proposed Unity Dam project. Jordan's dispute with Saudi Arabia over shared ground-water is no nearer resolution: Jordan's precarious financial position especially in the post-Gulf War period, limits its ability to demand concessions on sustainable exploitation of the Disi aquifer.

Water issues are on the agenda of current multilateral peace talks: the Israeli negotiating position is based on technical cooperation set against Arab, particularly Jordanian and Palestinian, demands for gestures of political goodwill and recognition of usage rights. The water factor is clearly an obstacle to potential territorial concessions by Israel. On this basis the most that could be achieved in the initial stages is cooperation on the exchange of hydrological information, still regarded as politically sensitive, and, perhaps eventually, the establishment of a regional technical committee on water management. Progress is ultimately conditional on agreements on territory and sovereignty in general, on the delimitation of national and international borders, and on the extent of Palestinian autonomy or self-government.

In the Tigris–Euphrates region water supplies are more abundant but many similar environmental and economic constraints apply. In Turkey, Syria and Iraq, water is being used in multipurpose dam projects for power generation and for large-scale, water-intensive irrigation schemes. Water is not yet being treated as a commodity in any of these states and supplies to farmers are still heavily subsidized. Syria and (pre-war and eventually post-sanctions) Iraq are pursuing policies of food security despite poor economic returns, environmental degradation and bureaucratic obstacles, but will nonetheless continue to depend on high levels of food imports. Water-recovery methods, and improvement and maintenance of irrigation and municipal networks have not yet been given priority.

The anxieties surrounding Turkey's GAP project must be put into perspective. The project is intended primarily as a means of boosting economic development in Turkey's least developed and mainly Kurdish region, and has raised expectations of economic transformation. There is no doubt that the flows of the Tigris and Euphrates downstream will be reduced, but the timing is by no means certain, given funding and additional infrastructural development which will determine how efficiently the water is used. Iraq and Syria are constructing additional water storage facilities to offset likely depletions.

The extent to which water becomes an instrument of foreign policy and an item in international relations in this area depends principally on Turkey's security concerns and objectives, for as well as being the upstream state on the Tigris and Euphrates it also has the strongest military capability. Furthermore, Turkey's economic ties with the Middle East have become relatively less important since the mid-1980s, so it is somewhat less vulnerable to economic pressure from its downstream neighbours.

It is unlikely that disputes between Turkey and Syria, Turkey and Iraq, or Syria and Iraq over exploitation of the Tigris and, especially, the Euphrates rivers would escalate beyond diplomatic protests. Water issues occupy a relatively minor position on the regional security agenda compared to the question of Kurdish autonomy and the activities of nationalist movements like the PKK. Turkey's principal concern is the security of its southern and eastern borders and it has guaranteed minimum Euphrates flows into Syria. Turkey has indicated its willingness to participate in joint hydrological projects and to continue regular exchanges of hydrological data, but there will be no multilateral quota-based water sharing. Turkey's reluctance is partially explained by its insistence that it has sovereignty over water resources originating in its territory, and partially by Syria's own ambiguous position on the rights and obligations of riparian states. Syrian exploitation of the Yarmouk and, particularly in this context, the Asi (Orontes) river, is barely cooperative; Syria appears to have awarded itself the kind of upstream rights of sovereignty over these rivers which it vigorously denies to Turkey on the Euphrates or Tigris. There are as yet no internationally agreed or ratified legal principles which might settle this controversy. The only factor which modifies this position is that failure to reach agreement directly influences the volume of investment in the region by international financial institutions.

The Kurdish position on the region's water resources has not yet extended beyond general claims to sovereignty. The PKK has made actual threats against Turkey's hydraulic installations, especially the Atatürk dam. At the same time it has not proposed an alternative economic programme for the region, much less a water-management strategy.

Turkey's plans for exporting water for hard currency have been scaled down. The Peace Pipeline, involving as it did not only Syria and Iraq but also Jordan, Israel, Saudi Arabia and the Gulf states, has been rejected by proposed consumers and, in effect, by the Demirel administration in Turkey. However, smaller scale water exports, to Israel for example, are still under consideration.

Whilst sabotage of dams and related facilities cannot be ruled out in the Tigris–Euphrates region, the primary significance of water in interstate relations is clearly as a bargaining tool; it is a deterrent but not a practicable means of coercion. Syria and Iraq are aware that Turkey's position cannot be readily challenged militarily and that cooperation on water issues depends on the handling of the Kurdish question. So long as bilateral discussions on security and technical discussion on water management continue, the threat to stability is minimized.

In the Nile valley the issues of water supply and control are mainly of concern to Ethiopia, Sudan and, above all, Egypt. Environmental and economic factors relating to water policy are more significant in this region than questions of sovereignty or water rights. The latter are of principal interest to Egypt, although these are unlikely to be jeopardized by the activities of Egypt's upstream neighbours. The most serious problem facing the Nile basin states is the long-term unpredictability of Nile flows, vividly demonstrated by the drought of 1980–87.

Egypt's policy of agricultural expansion, which aimed at providing a large measure of self-sufficiency in food production, cannot possibly be sustained on this basis. The only way to reduce water consumption is to cut back on the amount of irrigated agriculture and, in the short term, to invest in water-saving methods by rehabilitating and maintaining irrigation and municipal water networks. However, the creation of agricultural growth and land reclamation areas is also an important means of population dispersal and job creation. The implementation of water-pricing schemes is extremely controversial in Egypt; resistance to water pricing is strong and alternative methods of cost recovery (through indirect taxation) do not encourage conservation for the right reasons. Agricultural policy has hitherto been highly interventionist and has subsidized urban consumers. Wide-ranging controls on the farming practices of the rural population are only gradually being phased out under present IMF-backed liberalization policies. These are structural problems which lie at the heart of the water debate in this area.

Securing the flow of Nile water is one of Egypt's principal strategic concerns, as it is entirely dependent on the river for its water supplies. Egypt is consequently concerned with political developments to the south. Its relations with Sudan have deteriorated steadily since the coming to power of the Bashir regime, especially over the issue of Sudanese support for Islamic groups in Egypt. However, the 'unity of the Nile valley' remains an enduring *leitmotif* in Egyptian–Sudanese relations, and there is no question of Sudan, Ethiopia or Eritrea interrupting the flow of the Nile for hydraulic projects in the short to medium term on a scale which Egypt could realistically consider threatening.

Integrated, rather than competitive, Nile basin management is advocated by many hydrologists, for example through the development of reservoirs in the Ethiopian highlands or on the Upper White Nile. Yet existing and prospective economic contacts between the riparian states are limited. The civil war in southern Sudan has indefinitely postponed the water recovery projects in the Sudd region, whose consequences for the local environment are in any case controversial. In Ethiopia, plans to develop the Blue Nile region are proceeding very slowly and, given that any future development would have to be financed by overseas aid, are unlikely to antagonize Egypt.

More positively, there is a good record of negotiations between the Nile riparians. The 1959 Egypt–Sudan Nile Waters Agreement remains the only working arrangement for water allocation in this area, and indeed in the Middle East in general. It is impossible to envisage any future agreements which would not continue to promote the primacy of Egypt's interests and Egypt has no immediate incentive to concede the advantageous terms of the 1959 Agreement. Ethiopia, as the principal contributor of Nile waters, will eventually demand a more powerful voice in discussions on water but is unlikely to seek direct confrontation with Egypt. These factors combine to produce an unsatisfactory status quo in the Nile valley, but not a long-term threat to regional stability.

The relationship between water availability and exploitation, and political stability in the Middle East may thus be evaluated on several levels. The starting point for analysis, and the core of the Middle East water crisis, is clearly national water-planning policy. It is a potential cause of instability but also the basis for solutions.

Each state in the Middle East is aware of a growing mismatch between population and resources, especially water. The water deficit can be attributed to a number of causes, but most frequently to maldistribution, inappropriate allocation and wastage. Existing or prospective water shortages can be seen as a threat to internal political stability especially if they also prompt fears of food shortages. The availability of water is determined to a significant extent by government policy towards specific interest groups, particularly the agricultural sector and rural populations, and military or family client groups. Water distribution is also determined by the extent to which water-planning decisions are influenced by specific government agencies or private contractors or targeted against regime opponents. The solution to water-supply constraints depends on the ability of governments to implement such policies as water pricing and the reduction of subsidies on water, staple foods and agricultural inputs. These policies clearly have a direct impact on population needs and living standards. Adverse economic consequences of such measures which may prompt internal unrest, to varying degrees, can be mitigated depending on the scale and timing of implementation and on the extent and form of compensation. These considerations also modify competition between states and their negotiating positions.

Water-resource management is demonstrably used as an instrument of foreign policy, but it must be emphasized that water-related disputes are a consequence of, rather than a catalyst for, deteriorating relations between states. No state in the Middle East wants to go to war over water, but there are real concerns over the equitability of distribution. The proximate cause of actual conflict over water would be the unilateral appropriation or diversion of a shared water course by an upstream riparian without consultation. Yet this is too simplistic a scenario and does not take into account the complex political and economic interrelationships between riparian states. Whilst military intervention can never be ruled out completely, cost is a deterring factor and there are no guarantees of achieving such objectives as the destruction of hydraulic installations and related infrastructure without serious domestic economic consequences.

Control over shared water resources will continue to be used to exert political pressure and the water factor is a useful reminder of dependency. Israel, Turkey and Egypt, however efficiently managed their national water policy, will continue to dictate the regional water agenda for the reasons stated. They have little incentive to concede what they regard as a strategic asset, namely priority usage. Whatever negotiations take place, it is unlikely that this strategic advantage will be significantly modified. Willingness to negotiate does, however, influence decisions on international backing for specific projects.

The long-term cooperative development of international water resources in the Middle East thus presents the greatest challenge to policy-makers within and outside the region. There has been a significant trend towards collaboration, even though this is largely confined to technical matters: cooperation on the exchange of hydrological data, flood forecasting, joint HEP and water-recovery ventures, for example. It is these small-scale confidence-building measures, combined with a re-evaluation of national water allocation, which are of interest to and indeed are encouraged by international financial and development institutions, possible aid donors or investors. These policies can dampen regional tension and contribute to stability. In the long term they might be extended to wider-ranging fluvial commissions or international conventions to include discussion on legal issues and possible joint ventures. These are objectives which are widely considered desirable, but they are only practicable so long as the water issue is not separated from its wider political context.

APPENDIX I: WATER IN OIL ECONOMIES

Although this Paper focuses on shared watercourses where the water factor plays a significant role in international relations, it is interesting to look briefly at water supply and national security in the oil-producing states of the Arabian Peninsula and in Libya. The Gulf states are using oil revenues to invest in desalination to supply drinking water (the region accounts for 60% of the world desalination capacity) and fossil ground-water for irrigated agriculture in order to boost domestic food production. In the mid-1980s Saudi Arabia was the third largest food importer, but in 1991 became the world's sixth largest exporter of wheat; wheat production is heavily subsidized, with guaranteed producer prices several times the world price and estimated annual water consumption of eight cubic kilometres.[1] In the 1980s the UAE and Kuwait invested in local fruit, vegetable and poultry production in order to achieve self-sufficiency. Oil revenues were enough to cover the large volume of regional food imports but economic considerations were outweighed by feelings of strategic vulnerability or the fear of the 'food weapon'. The drive for self-sufficiency is the single biggest drain on local water resources.

Libya has also adopted a grand strategy for boosting domestic food production, especially livestock feed, in a $27-bn water pipeline project. Libya's coastal, rechargeable aquifers have been severely overpumped, leading to large-scale saline water intrusion. There are large reserves of fossil water in the sparsely-populated south which are now being transferred to the coastal areas via the Great Man-made River (GMR) project. When all five stages of the project are completed the GMR is expected to convey $1.9km^3$ annually to the north, in part compensating for local aquifer depletion. At best this supply will last for 50 years, depending on how it is exploited. The Libyan government initially planned to use the water for desert reclamation, but there is evidence to suggest that this will be on a smaller scale than planned.[2]

TABLES

Table 1: Population Data

	mid-1991 estimate (m)	% urban mid-1990	natural % increase	2000 forecast (m)	2010 forecast (m)
Egypt	54.5	47.0	2.9	69.0	81.8
Ethiopia	53.2	13.0	2.9	70.8	93.6
Gaza	0.775		3.8	1.0	
Iraq	17.1	71.0	2.7–3.9	27.2	31.0
Israel*	4.9	2.0	1.6	5.4	6.1
Jordan	3.4	68.0	4.1	5.7	6.8
Lebanon	3.4	84.0	2.1	4.1	4.9
Sudan	25.9	22.0	2.9	33.6	44.0
Syria	12.8	50.0	3.8	18.0	25.9
Turkey	58.5	61.0	2.2	69.0	83.4
West Bank	1.25		3.9		1.7

Sources: Population Concern; Israel Central Bureau of Statistics, *Statistical Abstract of Israel 1991* (Jerusalem: 1991); Jordan Higher Council for Science and Technology, estimates 1991; UNDP, *Human Development Report* (Geneva: 1992); UNRWA estimates, Vienna, 1992; World Bank, *World Development Report 1992* (Washington DC: World Bank, 1992).

Note:
* Jewish population of Israel pre-1967 to end 1990 is estimated at 3.947m. Population growth depends on the level of immigration especially from the former Soviet Union. If 500,000 immigrants arrive by the year 2000 then the Jewish population is expected to reach 5.2m, If not it is forecast at 4.7m (estimates by Professor Arnon Soffer, University of Haifa). The population of the Golan Heights is estimated at 26,000 (*Statistical Abstract*, 1991).

Table 2: Agriculture land use and production significance in Middle East economies

	Total area m ha	Arable and permanently cultivated area m ha	Irrigated area m ha	% of GDP	% workforce
Egypt	100.145	3.10	2.585	19.7	40.5
Ethiopia	122.190	13.930	0.162	40.0	74.5
Gaza	0.038	0.018	0.011		16.4[a]
					20.4[b]
Iraq	43.832	5.450	2.550	19.7	20.5
Israel	2.077	0.437	0.206	7.6	4.2
Jordan	8.921	0.376	0.057	7.7	7.6
Lebanon	1.040	0.360	0.087	8.7	8.8
Syria	18.518	5.503	0.863	27.8	24.1
Sudan	250.581	12.510	1.890	36.0	60.2
Turkey	77.945	27.885	2.220	5.1	20.5
West Bank	0.58	0.16	0.01[c]		8.7[d]
			0.003[e]		29.5[f]

Sources: Food and Agricultural Organisation, *FAO Production Yearbook, 1991*, Rome, (various tables). State of Israel, Central Bureau of Statistics, *Statistical Abstract of Israel*, 1991. M. Benvenisti and S. Khayat, *West Bank Atlas* (Jerusalem: the West Bank Data Base Project), 1988).

Notes:

[a] Israel	[c] Palestine (1985 estimate)	[e] Settlers
[b] Gaza	[d] Israel	[f] West Bank

Table 3: The Food Gap

	Food imports $m (excl fish)	% total imports by value (1990)	Food exports $m	Cereal imports 100m tonnes	Cereal exports 100m tonnes	Cereal imports $m	Cereal exports $m
Egypt	2,698.3	31	270.0	85,798	821	1,455	20.52
Ethiopia	206.4	17	24.4	6,866	0	135.2	0
Gaza	30.2		90.5	1,360		1.3	
Iraq	1,353.2	15	49.2	28,344	6	566	0.35
Israel	940.1	7	974.8	18,025	15	279.22	0.49
Jordan	644.3	19	98.0	14,905	393	270.68	1.7
Lebanon	491.7		156.9	3,563	100	5.9	2.2
Libya	1,143.9	16	0	22,896	0	433.55	0
Saudi Arabia	3,383.9	15	354.6	52,743	15,090	877	212.88
Sudan	198.9	18	198.9	5,860	1,000	97.94	22
Syria	648.1	17	413.0	20,914	650	381	11.5
Turkey	1,371.4	7	2309.2	31,770	2,095	560	38

Source: Food and Agriculture Organization, *Production Yearbook*, 1991.

Table 4: Main water-related agreements

Nile

15 April 1891	UK, Italy	Demarcation of spheres of influence in East Africa
15 May 1902	UK, Ethiopia	Irrigation works on the Blue Nile
9 May 1906	UK, Congo	Protecting level of Lake Albert (upper White Nile)
13 Dec 1906	UK, France, Italy	Safeguarding British and Egyptian interests in the Nile basin
7 May 1929	UK (Sudan), Egypt	Nile Waters Agreement
23 Nov 1934	UK (Tanzania), Belgium (Rwanda, Burundi)	Kagera river agreement
May 1949	UK (Uganda, Kenya, Tanzania), Egypt	Owen Falls agreements
8 Nov 1959	Egypt, Sudan	Nile Waters Agreement

Tigris-Euphrates

23 Dec 1920	UK, France	Agreement on utilization of Tigris and Euphrates
29 March 1946	Turkey, Iraq	Treaty of Friendship and Good Neighbourliness
6 July 1987	Turkey, Syria	Protocol on economic co-operation

Jordan

3 Feb 1922	UK, France	Agreement on utilization of the Yarmouk
4 June 1953	Jordan, Syria	Agreement on utilization of the Yarmouk
3 Sept 1987	Jordan, Syria	Agreement on the utilization of the waters of the Yarmouk

Recent principal international legal deliberations

1959–	International Law Commission (UN)	Draft articles on non-navigable use of international watercourses*
September 1961	Institute of International Law	Salzburg Resolutions
August 1966	International Law Association	Helsinki Rules
March 1977	UN Conference on Water, Mar del Plata	

* Latest draft, 1991

Notes

Units

1 hectare (ha) – 2.4 *feddans*
1 hectare – 10 *dunams*
1 cubic metre (m³) – 1,000 litres

Water supply and consumption is expressed in million cubic metres (mcm). 1,000 million cubic metres = 1 billion mcm or 1 cubic kilometre (1 km³).

Introduction

[1] See, for example, T. Naff and R. Matson, *Water in the Middle East: Conflict or Cooperation?* (Boulder, CO: Westview Press, 1985), pp. 1–21; J. Starr and D. Stoll, *US Foreign Policy on Water Resources in the Middle East* (Washington, DC: CSIS, 1987); J. Starr and D. Stoll, 'Water for the year 2000' in J. Starr and D. Stoll (eds), *The Politics of Scarcity* (Boulder, CO: Westview Press, 1988), p. 149; E. Salameh, quoted in George Moffat III, 'By the year 2000 water, not oil, will be the dominant resource issue' *Christian Science Monitor*, 8 March 1990, p. 10.

[2] *Water Resources Planning to meet long-term demand: guidelines for developing countries*, United Nations Natural Resources: Water Series, 21. (New York: UN, 1988) pp. 69–70. The cost of surface irrigation is estimated at $500–700/ha, sprinkler irrigation at $900/ha and drip irrigation at $1,300–1,500/ha (on-farm systems only, headworks not included).

[3] See, for example, *Jerusalem Post*, 16 November 1991, *Arabies*, July/August 1990, p. 47.

Chapter I

[1] A. Soffer and N. Kliot, 'The Water Resources of the Jordan Catchment: Management Options', in British Society for Middle East Studies (BRISMES), *Annual Conference Proceedings, 1991*, pp. 205–10.

[2] *ibid.*

[3] Naff and Matson, (*op. cit.* in Introduction, note 1); *Science and Technology* (Arabic), July 1991; J. Kolars, *The Litani River in the Context of Middle East Water Resources*, paper presented to conference on Water Resources and Security in South Lebanon, Royal Institute of International Affairs (RIIA), London, 4 October 1991, p. 3. Kolars estimates annual Litani discharge as 920.153mcm based on data collected by Naff and Associates for Middle East Research at University of Pennsylvania.

[4] TAHAL, *Water Master Plan, Report on the Water Sector in Israel*, 1990.

[5] A. Soffer, 'Demography in Eretz-Israel: 1988 and the year 2000' in N. Beschorner and St J.B. Gould (eds), *Altered States: Israel, Palestine and the Future* (London: School of Oriental and African Studies, 1991); and 'Israel's Demographic Dilemma' in *The Middle East*, May 1992, p. 12. An influx of 1m immigrants could increase the Jewish population to 5.2m by the year 2000.

[6] State of Israel Office of the State Comptroller, *Report on Water Administration* (Jerusalem: 1990) (Hebrew).

[7] Estimates vary. 70 mcm/yr is the figure given by TAHAL (*op. cit.* in note 4) p. 2-1 to 2-4. 25mcm are used in summer by Israelis on the banks of the Yarmouk, and 45mcm are diverted into Lake Tiberias in winter. According to K.M. Malouf, *Peace and Water in the Middle East* (Washington, DC: unpublished report), Israel uses 180mcm from the Yarmouk.

[8] TAHAL (*op. cit.* in note 4), Ch. 2, on damage to the coastal aquifer and *Report on Water Administration* (*op. cit.*, note 6). Interview with Dan Zaslavsky, *Jerusalem Report*, 13 February 1992, p. 14.

[9] State of Israel, Central Bureau of Statistics, *Statistical Abstract of Israel*, 1991.

[10] R. Sexton, *Perspectives on the Middle East Water Crisis: Analysing Water Scarcity Problems in Jordan and Israel*, (Irrigation Management Network, Overseas Development Institute, London) p. 22.

[11] *Israel Economist*, May 1990; *World Water and Environmental Engineering*, March 1991, pp. 29–30.

[12] *Jerusalem Report*, 13 February 1992, p. 14.

[13] See *Jordan Times*, 15 February 1992 and *Jerusalem Post*, 28 February 1992 on damage caused to Israeli agricultural production by flooding.

[14] Economist Intelligence Unit (hereafter EIU), *Israel Country Profile 15, 1991–92*, (London: EIU, 1991) pp. 15ff on the decline in Israeli agriculture; EIU, *Israel Country Report*, no. 3, 1991, p. 13. See also Sexton, (*op. cit.* note 10), pp. 22–8.

[15] Interview with Professor Arnon Soffer, University of Haifa, 1 March 1992.

[16] *Water Resources Planning (op. cit.* in Intro note 2).

[17] Farmers are charged for 80% of irrigation water at $0.125, 20% at $0.20 and $0.26 for excess use. 40% higher rates apply in July and August. TAHAL (*op. cit.* in note 4), p. 9-12.

[18] Knesset Member Edna Solodar, *Jerusalem Post*, 6 March 1991 interviewed as a champion of farmers' rights.

[19] According to Soffer (*op. cit.* in note 15) only 240 mcm/yr can feasibly be recovered.

[20] One plant is in operation at Eilat to desalinate brackish water. Another is under construction at Ashdod on the Mediterranean coast.

[21] The Palestinian Hydrology Group estimates the West Bank's water potential as 176 mcm/yr surface and 724 mcm/yr ground-water. Interview, 5 March 1992.

[22] TAHAL (*op. cit.* in note 4), pp. 3-4; 3-5.

[23] *Ibid.*, p. 3-5.

[24] Interviews at UN Development Programme (hereafter UNDP), East Jerusalem, 5 March 1992. This is another area in which statistics are controversial. According to TAHAL (*op. cit.*, in note 4), p. 3-4, 62% of Palestinian households have access to domestic taps, 14% to courtyard taps and 19% to courtyard cisterns. 5% only have access to communal water sources. According to TAHAL 'ample ground-water satisfies all regional requirements'. The Palestinian Hydrology Group contends that 51% of Palestinian villages have no access to running water.

[25] TAHAL (*op. cit.* in note 4) estimate. M. Benvenisti and S. Khayat, *West Bank Atlas* (Jerusalem: the West Bank Data Base Project (hereafter WBDBP), 1988), p. 26 estimated Palestinian water consumption as 115 mcm/yr, of which 100mcm went to agriculture. Israeli settlements were allotted 40–50 mcm/yr

including the 30 mcm/yr used in the Jordan valley.

[26] United Nations Relief and Works Administration (hereafter UNRWA) Information Department, May 1992. The number of Israeli settlers on the West Bank is estimated at 110,000 by UNRWA.

[27] Interviews at UNDP, East Jerusalem, 5 March 1992.

[28] *International Herald Tribune*, 14 May 1992.

[29] Interview with Palestinian Hydrology Group, 5 March 1992.

[30] According to the Palestinian Hydrology Group (*ibid.*) the irrigated area was 27% in 1967. Macro-economic changes on the West Bank – closer links with the Israeli economy – labour migration, dumping of subsidized Israeli goods on West Bank markets are also attributable. The picture has changed to some extent since the *intifada*, as a result of restrictions on labour movements and Arab boycotts and strikes, but structural dependence remains. Harvesting, transport and sale of agricultural produce have been adversely affected by curfews.

[31] WBDBP (*op. cit.*, in note 25); and D. Kahan, *Agriculture and Water Resources in the West Bank and Gaza 1967–87*, (Jerusalem: WBDBP, 1987).

[32] J. Dillman, 'Water Resources in the Occupied Territories' in *Journal of Palestine Studies*, Autumn 1989, Vol. XIX no. 1, p. 26; Interviews at UNDP, East Jerusalem, 5 March 1992.

[33] Water Department of the Military Government of the West Bank, *Monthly Discharge of Underground Water in Yehuda and Shomron, 1977–8*; and T. Ataov, 'Israel's Use of Palestinian Waters' in I. Abu-Lughod, (ed), *Palestinian Rights: Affirmation and Denial* (Wilmette, Illinois: Medina Press, 1982), pp. 152–335.

[34] *Jerusalem Report*, 1 August 1991.

[35] State of Israel Office of the State Comptroller, *Report on Water Administration*, (Jerusalem, 1985).

[36] Interview with Dan Zaslavsky, 4 March 1992.

[37] WBDBP (*op. cit.* in note 25).

[38] UN Economic and Social Commission for West Asia (ESCWA), September 1991 Report, *Israeli land and water practices in the occupied*

Palestinian and other Arab territories, (Amman: UN-ESCWA, 1991), pp. 11 and 22.

[39] UNRWA, March 1992. Population density in the Gaza Strip is 3,800/km². See H.J. Bruins, A. Tuinhof and R. Keller, (1991) *Water in the Gaza Strip,* Government of the Netherlands, Ministry of Foreign Affairs, Directorate-General for International Cooperation, 1991.

[40] *Ibid;* Abu Maila, S. Yusuf, 'Water Resource Issues in the Gaza Strip', *Area,* 23 March 1991, pp. 209–16.

[41] TAHAL (*op. cit.* in note 4), p. 3-5.

[42] Water quality is defined according to the quantity of dissolved solids, especially chlorides, in the watercourse or aquifer and is measured as parts per million (ppm) or milligramme per litre (mg/l). The most harmful minerals are magnesium sulphate, magnesium chloride, sodium sulphate, sodium carbonate and sodium chloride. The World Health Organisation has set a drinking-water guideline of 250mg/l.

[43] ESCWA estimates: 80mcm/yr irrigation, 21mcm/yr domestic use (*op. cit.* in note 38), p. 4.

[44] Z. Schiff, *Security for Peace: Israel's Minimum Security Requirements in Negotiations with the Palestinians,* Washington Institute Policy Paper No. 15 (Washington DC: Washington Institute for Near East Policy, 1989), p. 22.

[45] S. Roy, *Gaza Strip Survey* (Jerusalem, WBDBP, 1987).

[46] Jordan Higher Council for Science and Technology estimate, 1991. The Hashemite Kingdom of Jordan, Ministry of Water and Irrigation Water Authority, 'Jordan's water resources and expected domestic demand by the years 2000 and 2010'.

[47] Interview at Jordan Ministry of Water and Irrigation, 10 February 1992.

[48] M.M. Abu Ajamieh, F.K. Bender, and R.N. Eicher, *Natural Resources in Jordan,* Ministry of Energy and Mineral Resources, 1988, pp. 148, 150; and interviews at Higher Council for Science and Technology, 12 February 1992.

[49] Total cultivated area: 582,300ha; irrigated: 59,000ha of which 26,700 are in the Jordan valley. The cultivated area accounts for 6% of the total land area.

[50] EIU, *Jordan Country Profile* (London: EIU, 1991).

[51] Interview with Dr Munther Haddadin, Regional Office for Integrated Development, Amman, 11 February 1992.

[52] Interviews with Minister for Water and Irrigation, Dr Samir Kawar, 10 February 1992 and at Jordan Higher Council for Science and Technology, 11 February 1992.

[53] Soffer and Kliot, (*op. cit.* in note 1); and Malouf, (*op. cit.* in note 7).

[54] Saa'd al-Din Mudallal, 'Water Resources in Lebanon' in *Science and Technology* (Arabic), July 1989; pp. 178–87.

[55] EIU, *Lebanon Country Profile 1990* (London: EIU, 1990); and Kolars, (*op. cit.* in note 3).

[56] Saa'd al-Din Mudallal (*op. cit.* in note 53), pp. 178–87.

[57] T. Naff and Matson, (*op. cit.* in Introduction, note 1), p. 63.

[58] *ibid.,* pp. 69 *ff.*

[59] *Jerusalem Report,* 12 March 1992, p. 24.

[60] Abba Eban quoted in S. N. Saliba, *The Jordan River Dispute* (The Hague: Martinus Nijhoff, 1968), p. 9.

[61] Saliba (*ibid.*), p. 24.

[62] Saliba (*ibid.*), p. 26.

[63] *Foreign Relations,* 1953–55 Vol. XIV *Memo of Conversation, Department of State,* 11 July 1955.

[64] D. Wishart, 'The Breakdown of the Johnston Negotiations over the Jordan Waters', *Middle Eastern Studies,* vol. 26, no. 4, October 1990.

[65] Naff and Matson (*op. cit.* in Introduction, note 1), p. 42.

[66] Interview with Dr Munther Haddadin, (*op. cit.* in note 50).

[67] Solar water heaters on Palestinian homes were regarded as legitimate targets for reprisals by Israeli forces during the suppression of the *intifada.*

[68] E. Salameh, 'Effects of the Mediterranean–Dead Sea Canal on Jordan's Groundwater Resources' in A. Farid and M. Sirriyeh (eds), *Israel and Arab Waters* (London: Arab Research Centre, 1985)

[69] See also A. M. Garfinkle, *Israel and Jordan in the Shadow of War* (Basingstoke: Macmillan Press, 1992), p. 81. The argument about detrimental

rises in sea level and other damage is not entirely convincing.

[70] *Jerusalem Report*, 16 April 1992.

[71] Z. Schiff (*op. cit.* in note 43), pp. 17–24

[72] *Jerusalem Post*, 18 August 1990.

[73] E. Kally in G. Fishelson (ed.), *Economic Cooperation in the Middle East* (Boulder, CO: Westview Press, 1989); H. Shuval, *Approaches to solving water resource conflicts in arid areas: Israel and her neighbours as a case study*, Paper given at 2nd Consultation of the WHO/FAO Working group on legal issues in water supply and waste water management – World Health Organization, Geneva, 10–12 September 1991.

[74] *Jerusalem Report*, 13 February 1992.

[75] Palestinian Hydrology Group/Palestinian Advocates Group. Case submitted to International Water Tribunal, Amsterdam, February 1992. Palestine National Council, Algiers, November 1988, resolution called for the 'return to full Palestinian Arab sovereignty of all natural resources specifically land and water'.

[76] Interview with HRH Crown Prince Hassan of Jordan. HRH stressed the importance of seeking a regional idiom as the basis for multilateral negotiations, 12 February 1992.

[77] Letter to Lord Curzon, 30 October 1920, quoted in S. Bardawil, *Israel's Claim on Lebanese Waters: The Litani River*, unpublished M.Phil dissertation, May 1991, St Antony's College, Oxford, p. 15.

[78] Kolars, (*op. cit.* in note 3), and T. Naff, 'Israel and the Waters of South Lebanon', paper presented to Conference on Water and Security in South Lebanon, RIIA, London, 4 October 1991.

[79] Interview with Professor Arnon Soffer, University of Haifa, 1 March 1992.

Chapter II

[1] D. McDowall, *The Kurds, a Nation Denied* (London: Minority Rights Group, 1992), p. 12.

[2] For details of river flow, see J. Kolars, 'The Future of the Euphrates River', World Bank Workshop, June 1991, Washington DC, and J. Kolars and C. Mitchell, *The Euphrates River and the South-East Anatolia Development Project*, (Carvondale: University of Southern Illinois Press, 1991).

[3] Interview with Dr Özden Bilen, DSI State Hydraulic Works, Turkey, 24 February 1992.

[4] A.I. Bağis, *GAP: The Cradle of Civilisation Regenerated*, (Ankara: Interbank, 1989), p. 45.

[5] Interviews with Dr Seyfi Tashan, Foreign Policy Institute, Ankara and Dr Özden Bilen, DSI, 24 February 1992.

[6] Bağis, (*op. cit.* in note 4), pp. 62–3; EIU, *Turkey Country Report No. 4 1991* (London: EIU, 1991), p. 3. See also J. Kolars, 'The Hydro-Imperative of Turkey's Search for Energy', *Middle East Journal*, Winter 1986, Vol. 40, no. 1, pp. 53–67.

[7] GAP Master Plan. Interview with Dr Servet Mutlu, Vice-President, GAP, 21 February 1992.

[8] *Ibid.*

[9] *Die Zeit*, 20 December 1991.

[10] UNDP Project Document Syr/90/001/A/01/99: *Improved Management of Water Resources for Agricultural use* (Damascus, 1991).

[11] *International Herald Tribune*, 16–17 November 1991.

[12] Interviews, Syrian Ministry of Irrigation, 20–21 February 1991; and Dr Zuheir Farah Abu Daoud, *Arab Researcher*, April–June 1990. Proceedings of Round Table Conference on the Euphrates river, Arab Research Centre, London, February 1990.

[13] UNDP Project Document (*op. cit.* in note 10).

[14] See J. Hannoyer, *Maghreb-Machrek*, July–August–September 1985, pp. 24–42 on local responses to state projects and dislike of state/urban intervention.

[15] EIU, *Syria Country Profile, 1990–91* (London: EIU, 1991); *Middle East Economic Digest*, 17 April 1992.

[16] EIU, *Iraq Country Profile, 1990–1*, (London: EIU, 1991), p. 21.

[17] Main water storage projects in Iraq are dams at Dokan and Samarra on the lesser Zab, Himrin on the Euphrates, Darbandikhan on the Diyala and Abu Dibbis storing a total of 120km^3. Additional projects were to add 45km^3. EIU, *ibid.*, p. 21.

[18] *The Middle East Review 1991–2*, (Saffron Walden, World of Information, 1991), p. 65.

[19] See *Report of the Mission of Prince Saddrudin Agha Khan, July 1991* (New York: UN, 1991); *World Water and Environmental Engineering*, September 1991, p. 9.

[20] *Middle East Economic Digest*, 1 May 1992, p. 14.

[21] *Middle East Economic Digest*, 6 March 1992, p. 16, quoting Baghdad municipal authorities.

[22] BBC, *Summary of World Broadcasts*, ME 1342 A/12, 30 March 1992.

[23] BBC, *Summary of World Broadcasts*, ME 1358, 17 April 1992, p. i.

[24] E. Picard, *Les relations entre la Turquie et ses voisins arabes: des contraintes idéologiques à celles de la géostrategie*. Colloque de Strasbourg sur la Turquie, November 1990.

[25] Masoud Barzani, *Turkish Daily News*, 25 February 1992.

[26] *Middle East Economic Survey*, 7 October 1991. In June 1991 the Iraqi Foreign Minister, Tariq Aziz, visited Ankara to request the reopening of the pipelines, but was met with a demand for vastly inflated transit fees and operating costs.

[27] Saliba, (*op. cit.* in Ch. I, note 59) p. 59.

[28] E. Kienle, *Ba'th versus Ba'th, Syrian-Iraqi Relations since 1968* (London: I.B. Tauris, 1990), pp. 96–100.

[29] *Protocol on Matters Pertaining to Economic Cooperation between the Republic of Turkey and the Syrian Arab Republic*, Official Gazette, Turkey, 1987.

[30] Presentation by Wassam al-Zahani (Iraqi spokesperson) to Round Table Conference (*op. cit.* in note 12).

[31] *The Middle East*, August 1991, p. 29, and *South*, August 1991, p. 14.

[32] BBC, *Summary of World Broadcasts*, ME 1221 A/10, 5 November 1991.

[33] Turkey now proposes to divert water from the Seyhan and Ceyhan rivers into the water-deficient Hatay area.

Chapter III

[1] See, for example, J.A. Allan, 'Review of Evolving Water Demands and National Development Options' in J.A. Allan and P.P. Howell (eds), *The Nile, resource evaluation, resource monitoring, hydropolitics and legal issues* (London: SOAS, 1990), pp. 181–192; J.A. Allan, 'The Nile Basin: The Need for an Integrated Water Management Programme' in G. Nonneman (ed.), *The Middle East and Europe: an Integrated Communities Approach* (London: Federal Trust for Education and Research, 1992), pp. 229–38.

[2] C. Gischler, *Water Resources in the Arab Middle East and North Africa* (Wisbech: Middle East and North Africa Studies (hereafter MENAS) Press, 1981); P. Beaumont, G.H. Blake and J.M. Wagstaff, *The Middle East: Geographical Study* (Chichester: John Wiley, 1988).

[3] Gischler (*ibid.*); and Beaumont, Blake and Wagstaff, (*ibid*).

[4] A.K. Biswas, Water Research Centre, Oxford, 1991, p. 38.

[5] Biswas (*ibid.*); H. Ayeb (1990) 'La necessaire revolution hydraulique en Egypte', in *Revue Tiers Monde*, no. 121 January–March 1990; R. Stoner, 'Future Irrigation Planning in Egypt' in Allan and Howell (*op. cit.* in note 1), pp. 83–92; P. Chesworth, 'History of Water Use in Egypt' in Allan and Howell (*op. cit.* in note 1) pp. 40–58.

[6] Central Bank of Egypt and IMF estimates, July 1992, quoted in *Middle East Economic Digest*, 11 September 1992.

[7] *ibid.*

[8] Interview with Dr M. Abu Zaid, Chairman, Water Research Centre, Egypt, 2 February 1991; *al-Hayat*, 22 January 1992.

[9] Evaporation from Lake Nasser ranges from 6–$13 km^3$/yr depending on lake volume, five times the annual water supply of Jordan, for example. Evaporation rates in the area are three metres/yr; one metre/yr in the Ethiopian highlands by comparison.

[10] Biswas (*op. cit.* in note 4), p. 22.

[11] *al-Hayat*, 22 January 1992.

[12] See Beaumont, Blake and Wagstaff (*op. cit.* in note 2), p. 524. Interviews at Desert Research Centre, Cairo, 4 February 1992. The water table in the oasis of al-Kharga fell rapidly from 30 to 100 metres below ground level as a result of inappropriate siting of wells. The New Valley project failed to attract significant settlers from the Nile valley and local infrastructure remains inadequate.

[13] Interviews, Desert Research Centre, Cairo, 4 February 1992.

[14] Ayeb (*op. cit.* in note 5), p. 85.

[15] *al-Hayat*, 5 January 1992.

16 Interview with Dr Hassan al-Khidr, Director, Economic Section, Ministry of Agriculture, Egypt, 1 February 1992.
17 *Al-Ahram*, 25 October 1991.
18 *Egypt Focus*, November 1992, p. 11.
19 EIU, *Egypt Country Profile 1990–91*, (London: EIU, 1991), p. 20.
20 Malouf, (*op. cit.* in Ch. I, note 7); P.P. Howell and M. Lock, 'The Control of the Swamps of the Southern Sudan' in J. A. Allan (ed.), *The Nile* (London: Routledge, forthcoming); R.O. Collins, *The Waters of the Nile* (Oxford: OUP, 1988).
21 D. Knott and R.G.M Hewett, 'Future Water Development in Sudan' in Allan and Howell (*op. cit.* in note 1), pp. 93–105.
22 *ibid.*, p. 95.
23 EIU, *Sudan Country Profile 1991–2*, (London : EIU, 1992), pp. 16–17.
24 Howell and Lock (*op. cit.* in note 20).
25 B. Kabanda and P. Kahangire 'Irrigation and Hydropower Potential and Water Needs in Uganda: An Overview' in Allan and Howell (*op. cit.* in note 1), p. 125.
26 The African Development Bank financed a pre-feasibility study to develop HEP (60,000MW) in Zaire and to construct an electricity grid linking Zaire to Uganda, Sudan, Egypt, Jordan, Syria, Turkey and possibly Western Europe. Egyptian Ministry of Electricity, 3 February 1992. Meeting held in Cairo, July 1992 between Egypt and Zaire on $4m feasibility study.
27 Z. Abate, *Planning and national water policy in Ethiopia* (London: World Bank, 1992).
28 *Ibid.*
29 *Ibid.*
30 *Ibid.*
31 J. Waterbury 'Ethiopie, la grande inconnue', in *Bulletin du CEDEJ*, September 1987, p. 37.
32 Professor J.A. Allan, personal communication; D. Whittington and G. Guariso, 'Implications of Ethiopian Water Development for Egypt and Sudan', *Water Resources Development*, vol. 3, no. 2, p. 133.
33 Professor J.A. Allan, personal communication.
34 *Petroleum Economist*, 24 April 1992, and *al-Hayat*, 6 and 7 April 1992.
35 Waterbury (*op. cit.* in note 31), p. 37.
36 Professor J.A. Allan, personal communication.
37 Whittington and Guariso (*op. cit.* in note 32).

Appendix I

1 See *Die Zeit*, 20 December 1991, pp. 14–15.
2 J.A. Allan, 'Water Resource Evaluation and Development in Libya' in *Libyan Studies*, 1989, no. 20: pp. 235–42.